# IN PURSUIT OF
# DEVON'S HISTORY
## A GUIDE FOR LOCAL HISTORIANS IN DEVON

compiled by

Ian Maxted
County Local Studies Librarian
Devon Library and Information Services
in association with
The Devon History Society

## DEVON BOOKS

First published in Great Britain in 1997

British Library Cataloguing in Publication Data
CIP record for this book is available from the British Library

ISBN 086114 917 3


DEVON BOOKS
Official Publisher to Devon County Council
Halsgrove House
Lower Moor Way
Tiverton
Devon EX16 6SS
Tel: 01884 243242
Fax: 01884 243325

*The cover illustration is taken from George Bickham's 1796 map
'Devonshire', part of his series entitled 'A Curious Antique Collection of
Birds-Eye Views'* (Westcountry Studies Library)

Printed in Great Britain by BPC Information Ltd, Exeter.

# CONTENTS

# INTRODUCTION

For a number of years I compiled leaflet guides to various aspects of the local studies library resources in Devon and it had long been my intention to expand and improve these. The wish of The Devon History Society to produce a guide to local studies research in Devon has provided the opportunity both to integrate and extend the coverage of information in these leaflets. The present work has therefore relied heavily both on my own previous guides and on guides produced by the Devon Record Office and others. Some sections of this guide have been revised and indeed written by other members of The Devon History Society and I am most grateful to them for their assistance. The section on local history societies for example is almost entirely written by Adrian Reed and I am also grateful to Margery Rowe, Simon Timms, Todd Gray and others for their advice. From my position as a librarian I have not been able to develop the sections on archival and some other sources as much as I would have liked in the time available and this has undoubtedly resulted in some unevenness in coverage. I hope that this first attempt to provide a guide to local historians in Devon will well used and result in a flood of suggestions for improvement in the next edition.

Ian Maxted
County Local Studies Librarian
September 1997

# ABBREVIATIONS

DCRS    Devon and Cornwall Record Society

DRO     Devon Record Office

IGI     International Genealogical Index

LHS     Local History Society

PRO     Public Record Office

WSL     Westcountry Studies Library

# REFERENCING

Each chapter of this work is divided into sections and sub-sections. For instance Part 3 contains section 3.1 **Published Sources**, followed by subsection 3.111 **Newspapers** and subsection 3.112 **Periodical Articles**, and so on. Each section and subsection appears in the Contents list on pages 3 and 4, and also in the index where subjects are listed in alphabetical order. The symbol below appears at the head of every page providing a ready reference to the chapters.

# PART 1
# FIRST STEPS IN LOCAL HISTORY

There are a number of ways in which an interest in local history may be stirred. You may have seen a programme on the television, you may have moved into an interesting house or community, family history research may have led you to want to find out more about the places where your ancestors lived. For those who have developed an interest in local history but are not yet certain of the direction in which their interest could lead, there are a number of ways to find out more. There is much useful information, including addresses of organisations in *Local studies in Devon: a guide to resources*, a directory which is compiled and updated regularly by Devon Library Services.

1.1 LIBRARIES. The lending departments of most public libraries have at least one shelf of books of local interest. The subject classification number for the history of Devon is 942.35 and for description and travel 914.235. Books on special topics are often scattered by the classification scheme, for example books on Devon railways may be at 385.094235, but many libraries have gathered all books of local interest together regardless of subject. Public and non-public libraries are discussed further in section 2.1.

1.2 BOOKSHOPS AND PUBLISHERS. Most bookshops have a section of books of local interest, often adjoining the travel section. Secondhand and antiquarian booksellers likewise have shelves of local books and pamphlets. A number of booksellers produce catalogues specialising in local history. Prices vary, but are normally higher than could be expected from a local bookshop, as is often the case with antiquarian book fairs. Nevertheless they often have material which it would be difficult to track down locally. Auction sales occasionally have books of local interest but prices are often high and books are sold in lots which often include unwanted items. Among regional publishers who specialise in local publications are Devon Books, the University of Exeter Press, and Obelisk Publications. The national publishers Alan Sutton, Phillimore and Batsford have traditionally had a keen interest in local history publications. Section seven of *Local studies in Devon: a guide to resources* gives details of a selection of booksellers and publishers.

**1.3 PERIODICALS.** There are a number of periodicals you may wish to subscribe to. Some come as part of the membership of organisations (see section 1.4). Apart from the local publications such as *The Devon historian* or *Dartmoor magazine*, there are national titles which contain useful articles on methods of local history research as well as lists of events and publications. The two main titles are *Local historian* and *Local history magazine*. Section five of *Local studies in Devon: a guide to resources* gives the titles of the main local history periodicals.

**1.4 ORGANISATIONS.** If your interest deepens you may wish to join a local history organisation. The Devon History Society exists to provide a link between such organisations and, beside publishing *The Devon historian* twice yearly, it holds an annual conference in Exeter and meetings twice yearly in various parts of the county. Other relevant county organisations include the Devonshire Association, the Devon Archaeological Society and the Devon Family History Society. A list of local history groups together with contact details, whether or not they are affiliated to The Devon History Society, forms section four of *Local Studies in Devon: a guide to resources.*

**1.5 COURSES.** The one-off talks and visits run by these organisations may not go far enough for your interest and you may wish to undertake a course. These normally commence in the autumn and details can be found in newssheets produced by the local education authority, sometimes as a supplement to a local newspaper. Enrolment takes place in the public library or at other centres. Section eight of *Local studies in Devon: a guide to resources* lists some of the main contacts. Beside evening classes, conferences and courses in local and regional history are also run by the University of Exeter.

**1.6 STARTING YOUR OWN RESEARCH.** Once your interest has deepened to the extent that you have joined an organisation or enrolled on a course, you may be ready to begin your own research or join in a group project. The next sections outline the main sources that are available to you.

# PART 2
# RESOURCE PROVIDERS

There are a wide range of institutions which contain information on local history. The most important are libraries, record offices and museums. Most of these institutions do not have the staffing and resources to undertake research on your behalf, although they will be able to indicate material in their collections which may be of relevance to you. The Devon Record Office also operates a professional search service. To avoid wear and tear on fragile originals, much material in libraries and record offices is only available for consultation on microfilm or microfiche. This includes census returns, parish registers, newspapers, directories and maps. It is advisable to contact collections in advance to book a session on a microform reader.

Further reading:
Evans, D.Wyn, 'Local history collections in Devon', *Devon Historian* 20 (Oct 1982).
Centre for South Western Historical Studies. *Local historical studies guide* (regularly revised)

## 2.1. LIBRARIES

You will probably start your investigations at the nearest large local studies collection in the public library service.

### 2.11 PUBLIC LIBRARIES IN DEVON: MAIN LOCAL STUDIES COLLECTIONS
The four main collections in Devon all have specialist staff and separate accommodation for local studies material. They issue leaflet guides to their collections which give details of opening hours, collections and services. Information is also available to the public on the Internet: http://www.devon-cc.gov.uk/library/locstudy.html

WESTCOUNTRY STUDIES LIBRARY
Castle Street, Exeter EX4 3PQ. Tel: 01392-384216.
Devon's main local studies collection with detailed coverage of the four Western counties. Rich in early printed materials, it also houses the collections of the Devon and Cornwall Record Society.

PLYMOUTH LOCAL STUDIES LIBRARY
Drake Circus, Plymouth PL4 8AL. Tel: 01752-385909.
Concentrates on Plymouth, West Devon and Cornwall with good coverage of the rest of Devon. An important naval history collection is held here.

TORQUAY LOCAL STUDIES COLLECTION
Lymington Road, Torquay TQ1 3DT. Tel: 01803-386505.
Housed in the reference section of Torquay Central Library, this collection has good coverage of the South of Devon.

NORTH DEVON LOCAL STUDIES CENTRE
Tuly Street, Barnstaple. Tel: 01271-388607
Shares accommodation with the North Devon Record Office and the North Devon Athenaeum Library. It covers north Devon and Exmoor.

OTHER PUBLIC LIBRARY COLLECTIONS
Most branch libraries in the county hold some local studies material. This includes boxes of materials for neighbouring parishes copied from originals in the main collections. Some libraries, such as Exmouth, Newton Abbot and Bideford have considerable local studies collections.

LENDING COLLECTIONS
Material in the main collections is for reference only but lending copies of many titles are available through the county's lending libraries.

## 2.12 NON-PUBLIC LIBRARIES
Such libraries often have collections of local material but some are maintained by societies for members only and access may have to be arranged in advance. Details of non-public libraries are given in section one of *Local studies in Devon: a guide to resources*. The more important libraries include:

Devon and Exeter Institution. Tel: 01392-51017.
North Devon Athenaeum, Barnstaple. Tel: 01271-42174.
Torquay Natural History Society. Tel: 01803-293975.
University of Exeter Library: Tel. 01392-263263
University of Plymouth Library, Exmouth Campus.
Tel: 01395-255309

## 2.2 RECORD OFFICES

Information found in libraries may include references to manuscripts or archives. Archives are the records generated by institutions as part of their day-to-day activities. For these you will normally need to approach the local record office. Record offices hold archives of local authorities, businesses, estates and individuals. Devon's main Record Office is in Exeter (Tel: 01392-384253) with other offices in Plymouth (Tel: 01752-385940) and Barnstaple (Tel: 01271-388608). The Devon Record Office (DRO) also administers the Dean and Chapter archives of Exeter Cathedral and maintains a series of service points with micro-filmed copies of records in various parts of the county. Other archives of local significance are held in the Public Record Office (PRO), the House of Lords Record Office, the Duchy of Cornwall Record Office and indeed 'stray' archives can be found in widely scattered record offices. See section 3.3 for fuller details. Manuscripts of a non-archival nature can be found in record offices and local and national libraries such as the British Library and the Bodleian Library in Oxford.

Fuller details of record offices in the county are given in section two of *Local studies in Devon: a guide to resources*, published regularly by Devon Library Services.

## 2.3 MUSEUMS

There are some fifty museums in Devon with material on local history, including much printed and manuscript material as well three-dimensional artefacts. For details see guidebooks or directories, including section three of *Local studies in Devon: a guide to resources*. It is strongly advised to contact museums in advance, should you wish to view material which does not form part of the public displays.

# PART 3
# HISTORICAL SOURCES

This section is intended as a brief introduction to the sources for Devon's local history. There are various general guides to sources for English local history and on occasion courses are run locally which can give guidance on local and family history research.

Further reading:
Edwards, P. *Rural life: a guide to local records* (1993).
Campbell-Kease, J. *A companion to local history research.* (1989).
Hall, A.T. *Local history handlist.* 5th ed. Historical Association, 1982 (Helps for students of history; 69).
Hey, D. (ed). *The Oxford companion to local and family history.* (1996)
Hoskins, W.G. *Local history in Engand.* (1959).
O'Hea, Seamus. 'Some readily available sources for local historians in Devon' *Devon Historian*, 26 (April 1983), 11-17.
Richardson, J. *The local historian's encyclopedia.* 2nd ed. (1986).
Riden, P. *Local history: a handbook for beginners.* (1983).
Tiller, K. *English local history: an introduction.* (1992)

### 3.1 PUBLISHED SOURCES

Published sources are usually to be found in libraries while unpublished, archival sources are located in record offices. This does not necessarily mean that all published sources are secondary sources and only archives are primary sources. Sources such as newspapers and trade directories contain much information which can be found in no other source. Generally secondary sources and indexes should be consulted before the primary sources are tackled.

### 3.11 BIBLIOGRAPHIES

Bibliographies and catalogues of collections are the point of departure for all local studies research in Devon. They detail work previously undertaken and can avoid unnecessary duplication of research. Most titles listed here are available in the main libraries in the county and record offices and museums often hold reference copies.

Brockett, Allan. *The Devon Union List* (D.U.L.): *a collection of written material relating to the county of Devon* (1977). This is still one of the first places to check for most local studies searches. It lists some 8300 books to 1975 and is arranged alphabetically by author giving locations in six major collections in Exeter, Plymouth and Torquay. There is an alphabetical index in one sequence of places, subjects and persons. The compiler relied on records from contributing libraries, which were not always accurate, so the work should be treated with some caution. An annotated copy is kept in WSL.

*The Devon bibliography* published by The Devon History Society 1980-1984 and by Devon Library Services 1985 to date, aims to continue the Devon Union List but, while the detail of entries is fuller, it does not give locations. However most titles can be found in WSL, whose accessions form the basis of the list. To 1985 the arrangement was alphabetically by author, since 1986 it has been arranged by place subdivided by subject with author indexes. The period 1976-1979 is still to be covered.

Hoskins, W.G. *Devon* (1954) has an invaluable survey of the main sources consulted for this important work in the 'Bibliography' on pp.554-571. This has been updated in the commemorative edition of 1992 which also contains a list of Hoskins's own writings.

Davidson, James. *Bibliotheca Devoniensis: a catalogue of the printed books relating to the county of Devon* (1852). Supplement (1861). The earliest bibliography of the county and still the best for the early period as it lists many items which were lost in the air raids during World War II. Arranged in broad subject groupings with an author index, it gives some locations but WSL has Davidson's own annotated copy with fuller references. Most of Davidson's own collection, the Secktor Library, passed after his son's death to the Plymouth Athenaeum where it was destroyed in the blitz in 1942.

Plymouth Athenaeum. *Catalogue of the Davidson collection of pamphlets* (1894). Lists many items not included in *Bibliotheca Devoniensis*.

Maxted, Ian. *Books with Devon imprints: a handlist to 1800* (1989). Lists about 1200 books, pamphlets and single sheet items. Includes items now lost and hence not in the *Eighteenth century short title catalogue* as well as incorporating works listed in J. Ingle Dredge *A few sheaves of Devon bibliography* (1889).

### 3.111. Newspapers
*Bibliography of British newspapers. Cornwall*, edited by Jean Rowles; *Devon*, edited by Ian Maxted (1991). A comprehensive listing of several hundred titles from 1704 to date with detailed accounts of files in collections throughout the British Isles and abroad. There are notes of the local availability of microfilm and of indexes. This replaces Lorna Smith's *Devon newspapers: a finding list* (1975) which is more widely held and still a useful guide.

### 3.112. Periodical articles
There is no consolidated index of periodical articles relating to Devon although many libraries maintain partial card indexes and the Burnet Morris Index in the WSL (see 3.118) covers many periodicals up to 1940. *The transactions of the Devonshire Association* have a series of four indexes covering the first hundred volumes, *The Devon historian* has indexes to nos 1-15 and 16-30. The Library Association's county volumes of the *Subject index to periodicals* cover books and periodical articles for the years 1954-61 continued by the regional lists of their *British humanities index* 1962-66.

More general indexes will have to be consulted, such as the *British humanities index* after 1966, or the *Local studies index*. E.C.L.Mullins *A guide to the historical and archaeological publications of societies in England and Wales, 1901-1933* is also useful. The provision of a general index of periodical articles relating to Devon is something which should be addressed by a co-operative effort. A start has been made with a computerised index to major periodicals available in the larger local studies collections with print-outs in about twenty of the larger branch libraries. This can be consulted on-line in Devon's main local studies libraries.

### 3.113. Theses
Listings are to be found in *The Devon historian* no. 8 (1974), p.3-12, no.

9 (1974), p. 28-33 and no 16 (1978), p.27-30. Many local theses are held in the library of the University of Exeter or in individual departments. National listings include the *ASLIB index to theses*, available in major reference libraries.

### 3.114. Illustrations
Somers Cocks, J.V. *Devon topographical prints 1660-1870 : a catalogue and guide* (1977). Lists 3500 engravings and lithographs, arranged by place with a supplement listing in chronological order the sources from which many of the individual prints came. Locations are not given but many libraries keep copies annotated with their own holdings.

### 3.115. Archives
A useful guide to the main collections is DRO's *Brief guide, part 1: official and ecclesiastical* (1969). This is supplemented by annual reports and special lists on such subjects as *Parish, non-parochial and civil registers* and *Parish poor law records*. See section 3.3 below for details of other listings.

### 3.116. Local bibliographies
Only a selection for the major regions and towns are given here. A useful bibliography of parish and town histories, based on the holdings of WSL is: *Abbots Bickington to Zeal Monachorum* (Devon Libraries, 1994)

DARTMOOR
Hamilton-Leggett, Peter. *The Dartmoor bibliography* (1992). Seven thousand entries in two main sequences, each arranged alphabetically by author, one for books and the other for periodical articles. Locations are not given. The subject index is to broad subjects and places, making items on specific topics difficult to locate. About ten times the size of J.V.Somers Cocks *The Dartmoor bibliography: non-fiction* (1970-79).

EXMOOR
Miles, Roger. *The Exmoor bibliography: revised up to 31 December 1989* (1990). Replaces earlier editions of 1959 and 1965.

EXETER
Adams, Maxwell. 'An index to the printed literature relating to the antiquities, history and topography of the city of Exeter' *Trans. Dev. Assoc.* 33 (1901) p.270-308

PLYMOUTH
Worth, R.N. *The three towns bibliotheca* (1872-80). The three towns are Plymouth, Devonport and East Stonehouse.

TORBAY
Pike, John R. *Torquay, Torbay: a bibliographical guide* (1994), also his *Paignton, Torbay : a bibliographical guide* (1993) and *Brixham, Torbay: a bibliographical guide* (1993).

### 3.117. Subject bibliographies
These have been compiled on a wide range of topics or form part of works on specific subjects. Two examples for genealogical sources must suffice:

Raymond, S.A. *Devon: a genealogical bibliography* (2nd ed., 1994). Vol. 1: Sources; vol. 2: Family history. Includes much background information of general interest to local historians.

Peskett, Hugh. *Guide to the parish and non-parochial registers of Devon and Cornwall 1538-1837* (1977). An extremely full listing covering originals, transcripts and published versions, although many of the locations are out of date since the implementation of the Parochial Record Measure, and the DRO's list should also be referred to. See section 3.311 below.

### 3.118. Library catalogues and indexes
Some early catalogues have been published and may list items which have since disappeared from local collections, although they may still be available nationally in such locations as the British Library. Examples include:

Devon and Exeter Institution. *A catalogue of the library* (1850)
Royal Albert Memorial Museum, Exeter. *Catalogue of the reference library* (1901)
North Devon Athenaeum, Barnstaple. *Catalogue of the circulating and reference departments* (1898)
Plymouth Free Public Library. *Index catalogue of the reference department* (1892)

The current general catalogues of Devon Library Services and the Universities of Exeter and Plymouth are held on computer, sometimes with microfiche print-outs of all or part of the catalogues available. The University of Exeter's library catalogue includes works in the Devon and Exeter Institution and Cathedral libraries.

Large sections of the local studies collections are still only covered by card catalogues but work on computerisation of the local studies collections is well advanced, the resulting databases being available for consultation in the main local studies libraries on-line or through print-outs, and also on the Internet: http://www.devon-cc.gov.uk/library/locstudy.html.

Most libraries also have special information indexes. For example the card index in Plymouth Library covers a wide range of newspapers and periodicals. The most extensive card index in Devon local studies collections is the work of one man, the Recorder in Bibliography of the Devonshire Association: the Burnet Morris Index was compiled between 1915 and 1940 and contains over one million cards with detailed references to Devon persons, places and subjects. The arrangement is complex and a recent guide to the index is produced by Devon Library Services: *The Burnet Morris index ... : a guide* (1990).

### 3.12 HISTORIES
Histories can be located in catalogues under the author's name, if this has been ascertained from such sources as the bibliographies listed in section 3.11 above. In subject catalogues the arrangement varies. The standard Dewey number for Devon histories is 942.35 and its subdivisions, although relevant material can also be found under 914.235. In larger libraries there are either special adaptations of Dewey or alphabetical systems. For example in WSL histories are catalogued and shelved alphabetically by the place covered within each county.

### 3.121. County histories
Copies of the major county histories are to be found in the larger libraries in Devon with a selection in larger branches. Loan copies of some titles are available. Extracts from Polwhele and Lysons are frequently included in the parish packs which are available in most branch libraries and schools outside the major conurbations. The earliest of the county histories are essentially topographical surveys. These were compiled from the early 17th century onward. A useful survey of ten county histories is provided by A.A. Brockett 'The historians of Devon:

*[manuscript text]*

There are also *labourers*, that serve for daily wages, whereof be two sorts: the one is called a *spadiard*, a daily labourer in tin works, with whom there is no labourer in hardness of life to be compared; for his apparel is coarse, his diet slender, his lodging hard, his drink water, and for lack of a cup, he commonly drinketh out of his spade or shovel, or some such other thing.

*[manuscript text]*

THE common day-labourer, or hireling, as meanest, is last remembered. I speak of them that work by week or day in husbandry labour, or thereunto belonging, or in tin-works. Of the last are two sorts; one named a spador or searcher for tin, than whom (as it seems to me) no labourer whatsoever undergoes greater hazard of peril or danger, nor in hard or coarse fare and diet doth equal him: bread, the brownest; cheese, the hardest; drink, the thinnest; yea, commonly the dew of heaven; which he taketh either from his shovel, or spade, or in the hollow of his hand; as Diogenes, the cynic, was taught by a boy. He spends all day (or the major part thereof) like a mole or earth-worm undergound, mining in deep vaults or pits,

*The early histories copied extensively from each other. Illustrated are extracts relating to Dartmoor tinners from 17th century manuscripts held in the Westcountry Studies Library. (Top) Risdon's Chorographical description of the county of Devon, together with the 1811 printed edition and (bottom) Thomas Westcote's View of Devonshire, with the printed edition of 1845.*

a bibliographical appreciation' (1949), typescript, but available in Exeter and Plymouth. *Devon* by W.G. Hoskins (1954) also gives a summary in his bibliographical supplement.

There is no multi-volume history of Devon to compare with such authorities as Hasted for Kent or Collinson for Somerset. Only the first volume of the *Victoria county history of Devon* has appeared (1905) and this is confined largely to natural history and prehistory although it also has an edition of the Domesday Book.

Tristram Risdon, *The chorographical description or survey of the county of Devon* (1811, reprinted 1970). Begun in 1605 and finished in 1630, it circulated widely in manuscript, several versions being held in WSL. A mangled version was published by Curll (2 vol, 1714, reissued 1723, 1725, 1733). Before it was published *in extenso* in 1811 William Chapple began *A review of Risdon's survey of Devon* (1785, repr 1970) but only the first part was published before the author's death. Chapple's working copy is deposited in the DRO. It is confined largely to accounts of descents of estates. Apart from its own index, see: A.B.Prowse 'Index to Risdon's survey of Devonshire: personal names: edition of 1811' *Trans Dev. Assoc.* 26 (1894), 419-50.

Thomas Westcote, *A view of Devonshire in MDCXXX*, edited by George Oliver and Pitman Jones (1845). Like Risdon it is confined largely to accounts of descents of estates but is attractively written and is arranged according to the river valleys. Indexed in: A.B.Prowse 'Index to personal names in Westcote's view of Devonshire in 1630' *Trans. Dev. Assoc.* 27 (1895), 443-85.

Sir William Pole, *Collections towards a description of the county of Devon* (1791). Pole died in 1635 and most of his papers were destroyed in the Civil War. While incomplete, this publication is valuable as it is based on papers which have otherwise disappeared, but its interest is almost exclusively genealogical.

John Hooker, 'Synopsis chorographical of Devonshire' (1599). The earliest topographical account of Devon, this survives as British Library Harleian Ms 5827 of which a microfilm is available in WSL. There is also a version held in DRO. Extracts printed in *Trans. Dev. Assoc.* 47 (1915) p334-48. Used extensively by Westcote and Risdon.

Richard Polwhele, *The history of Devonshire* (3 vol 1797-1806, repr 1977). The most ambitious history attempted to date but incomplete and ramshackle. The general historical sections are of little value for the earliest period. The parochial descriptions are most useful for the south of the county but tail off badly.

Samuel and Daniel Lysons, *Magna Britannia. Vol 6: Devonshire* (2 vol, 1822). The best of the early county histories. Volume 1 contains a general introduction with useful accounts of industry and volume 2 parish histories. A major source for most later writers. It was based on extensive questionnaires held in manuscript in the British Library of which a microfilm is available in WSL.

Thomas Moore, *History of Devonshire* (3 vol, 1829-36). Incomplete as none of the intended parochial history appeared. A workmanlike text though inaccurate for the earliest periods. The second volume is made up of biographies, drawing extensively on John Prince's *Danmonii orientales illustres* (the second edition had appeared in 1811) and there are numerous good quality engraved plates.

Among early unpublished collections are those of Jeremiah Milles, Dean of Exeter from 1762 to 1784 in preparation for a book on Devon history. Milles circulated a questionnaire (see *Trans. Dev. Assoc.* 23, 154-57). The original returns are in the Bodleian Library but a microfilm copy of the completed questionnaires and a second series of 'parochial collections' is in WSL. See: B.F.Cresswell 'Milles' parochial collections for Devon' *DCNQ* 11 (1921), 320-4. In the Devon and Exeter Institution is to be found the Stockdale Collection of material gathered in preparation for a history of Devon which never appeared. The fullest index is provided by cards in the Burnet Morris Index in WSL (see section 3.118). The collection is discussed by Ian Stoyle in 'F.W.Stockdale: begetter of the Stockdale Collection' (*Devon historian*, 46, 1993, p.3-8).

Charles Worthy, *Devonshire parishes: or, the antiquities, heraldry and family history of twenty-eight parishes in the Archdeaconry of Totnes* (2 vol, 1887-89) is an example of a partial historical survey.

R.N. Worth, *A history of Devonshire* (1886). A readable and useful one-volume account, but 'not what we should call a history today' (Hoskins).

W.G. Hoskins, *Devon* (1954).   The best modern history of Devon, thematic rather than chronological, with a full gazetteer and valuable bibliography.   The second edition (1972) was not updated; a commemorative edition with an appreciation and a supplementary bibliography appeared in 1992.   Other works by Hoskins include *Old Devon* (1966) and *Devon and its people* (1959).   Hoskins did not cover Exeter in his general county history, *Devon*, for this see his *Two thousand years in Exeter* (1960 etc).

R. Stanes, *A history of Devon* (1985).   A good recent concise chronological introduction.

A listing of county histories and accounts of travel is given by Ian Maxted and Mark Brayshay in 'A list of of works on the topography of the south-west counties' in *Topographical writers in South-West England* (University of Exeter, 1996).

Further reading:
Curries, C.R.J. (ed). *A guide to English county histories.* (1997).

### 3.122. Town histories
Local studies libraries have good collections of town histories and branch libraries in the area covered by the histories normally have reference and frequently also lending copies.   The earliest published histories appear in the 17th and 18th centuries.   Examples are R. Izacke *Memorials of the city of Exeter* (1676) and Martin Dunsford *Historical memoirs of the town and parish of Tiverton* (1790).

Most early compilations have little on social history but reprint lists of office holders or texts of early charters and other documents or else they are annalistic in nature.   Recent town histories are frequently little more than collections of illustrations.   Even with publishers which specialise in local histories, individual volumes vary in the quality of historical research and interpretation and in the level of documentation provided.   Some towns, such as Cullompton and Crediton still have no large-scale published history, although the latter has a typescript compilation by T.W. Venn which is quite widely available.

### 3.123. Parish histories
Parish histories are usually to be found in the main local studies collec-

tions in the area where the parish is located and a copy is frequently to be found in the nearest branch. Many such histories are produced for limited circulation and it is not always possible to find lending copies.

The Parochial History Section of the Devonshire Association drew up guidelines for the compilation of parish histories, and a number were published from 1930 to the 1960s, e.g.
1. *Okehampton*, compiled by E.H. Young (1931)
2. *Holsworthy*, by W.I. Leeson Day (1934)

These are all arranged under a series of up to 38 main headings (e.g. manorial history, population, markets and fairs, education), many with subdivisions. H.F. Fulford Williams completed several dozen parish histories in typescript using the format drawn up by the Devonshire Association, and these are held in WSL. Also in WSL are folders of parish information compiled by the Devonshire Association in preparation for the publication of further histories, but most of these contain little material and they have not been added to for many years.

Local history groups and adult education classes sometimes produce parish histories. A recent example is: *Out of the world and into Combe Martin* (1989), a collection of essays by the Combe Martin Local History Group.

Many parishes still lack a printed history although much historical information can be found in such sources as the local church guide. A listing of town and parish histories held in WSL is available: *Abbots Bickington to Zeal Monachorum: a handlist of Devon parish histories* (Devon Library Services, 1994).

### 3.13 GUIDEBOOKS

Guidebooks are found in libraries, but the main libraries have often missed the more obscure local guides which can sometimes be found in museums or larger branch libraries. They are valuable for giving a picture of the locality at a particular point in time, often providing detailed information on local institutions and businesses as well as details of the major historical sites. Guidebooks were not published regularly in Devon until the early 19th century, partly the result of the French wars which closed the continent to those undertaking the Grand Tour and partly due to the cult of the picturesque which led people to seek out

# Wood's Fairhaven Hotel and Restaurant.

**Tariff:**

Boarding for one Person, including four meals with use of Dining Room, Drawing and Smoking Rooms,

FOR ONE PERSON

**5/6**

per day.

For TWO PERSONS

**10/-**

per day, inclusive.

*Hot Luncheons and Teas Daily.*

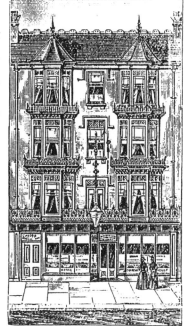

Boarding commences with the meal the Visitor arrives at, and is only charged to the meal he leaves at.

*Visitors going day trips are provided with late Dinner and Tea combined, on their return.*

Increased Dining, Drawing, Smoking and Bedroom accommodation.

DINING ACCOMMODATION FOR 100 PERSONS.

## 48, HIGH ST., ILFRACOMBE.

HENRY WOOD, Proprietor

Advertisements such as this appear frequently in local guidebooks and are sometimes more informative than the main text for the social historian. The advertisement for Wood's Hotel appeared in Twiss & Sons' illustrated guide to Ilfracombe *(1893)*.

beautiful landcapes in England. Early guidebooks furnish details of facilities such as hotels, assembly rooms and circulating libraries which were established in the coastal resorts. The arrival of the railways in the mid 19th century gave a boost to the publication of county guidebooks in such national series as Murray's or Ward Lock's. Local publishers include Besley of Exeter, Banfield of Ilfracombe and Croydon of Teignmouth. Many places, large and small have issued official guide-books for tourists in recent years. These are often undated and clues have to be sought in the advertisements which, in many cases, are among the most useful part of the contents for the social historian.

Prior to the 19th century not many people ventured far from home for pleasure. The journals of a dozen travellers from Leland in the mid-six-teenth century to Southey in the early nineteenth have been gathered together in *Early tours in Devon and Cornwall*, edited by R. Pearse Chope (1918, repr 1967). They often include vivid eye-witness accounts of towns and of the discomforts of travel.

### 3.14. DIRECTORIES

Directories are printed lists of local traders compiled for general sale by commercial publishers. They also frequently list private individuals and contain extensive information on the history, public institutions and major features of each community. The earliest directories cover London and were regularly published from the 1730s. Larger provincial towns begin to have their own directories from the later 18th century. Directories with national coverage begin to include Devon localities in Bailey's directory of 1783, and from 1822 for Devon they begin to be arranged within counties in Pigot's series of regional directories. Only larger towns were covered until Kelly's provincial directories began in the 1840s. The first directory in Devon to cover every parish is White's of 1850. Until the appearance of the final edition of Kelly's directory in 1939 county directories were published approximately every five years, providing a useful basis for tracing the development of communities. Kelly's directories were discontinued after 1939, a victim of the war and the growth of telephone directories, followed by most of their town directories in the 1970s, although local trade directories continue to be published, sometimes now having free distribution.

Most county directories are arranged by parish or town, either in one alphabetical sequence or sometimes within administrative areas such as

| | SHOPKEEPERS. | Sheers Wm. | TAILORS. |
|---|---|---|---|
| Norman John | Bale George | Southey Robert | Bragg Aaron |
| Talbot John | Jacobs Robert | Stradling Eliz. | Fry John |
| Taylor John | | | |
| White Thomas | | | |

DUNKESWELL, which gives name to a deanery, is a small village, in a narrow picturesque valley, near the source of a rivulet, 6 miles N.N.W. of Honiton. Its parish is boldly diversified with hill and dale, and comprises 536 souls, and about 4000 acres of land, including an open turf moor of 100 acres, and many scattered houses. Mrs. E. P. Simcoe owns a great part of the soil, and is lady of the manor. She has a pleasant seat at the south end of the parish, called *Wolford Lodge*, 4 miles N.N.W. of Honiton. This mansion was the seat of the late General Simcoe, and near it there was anciently a church, called *Wolfer Church*, which was granted by King John to DUNKESWELL ABBEY, which was founded at the north end of the parish, by Wm. Brewer, in 1201, for Cistercian monks, who were endowed with the manor and other lands, valued at the dissolution at £294. 18s. 6d. per annum. There are still some slight vestiges of the abbey, and on its site a handsome *District Church* has lately been erected by Mrs. Simcoe, in the Early English style, with several stained glass windows and a bell turret. She has endowed it with £50 per annum, and is patroness of the *perpetual curacy*, of which the Rev. T. Müller is the first incumbent. He is also incumbent of Dunkeswell perpetual curacy, valued at only £45, and in the patronage of Mrs. Mary Graves, the impropriator of the rectory and great tithes. The *Parish Church* (St. Nicholas,) is in the centre of the parish, about two miles south of the new Abbey Church. It was rebuilt in 1817, and is a small cruciform structure, with a tower and three bells. The *Wesleyans* have a neat chapel here, and the parish has a modern *School House*, in the Elizabethan style. *Peter Holway* left for the poor parishioners £100, which was laid out, in 1651, in the purchase of a house and 10a. of land ; the latter of which is let for £10, and the former was the parish workhouse. The poor have two yearly rent-charges, viz., 20s., left by *Charles Ford*, in the 25th of Elizabeth ; and 5s., left by *Nicholas Lacke*, in 1670. At an early date, *Nicholas Marke* left a yearly rent-charge of £5 out of Ashcombe estate, to be applied in apprenticing poor children. For schooling poor children this parish has about £1 yearly from *Mary Waldron's Charity.* (See Clayhidon.)

| | |
|---|---|
| Cox Thomas, blacksmith | **FARMERS.** |
| Kerby Thomas & Gosling Ann, *school* | Barton Thomas ‖ Bright David |
| Moon Wm. swine dealer | Burrough Robert ‖ Chinnick Wm. |
| Müller Rev Theodore, incumbent | Clement Francis ‖ Clement John |
| Parsons James, wheelwright | Critchett Hy. ‖ Derham Thos. *Abbey* |
| Salway Edw. tailor and parish clerk | Farrant Samuel ‖ Marks Samuel |
| Simcoe Mrs Elizabeth Posthuma, | Paul John ‖ Rosier Roger |
| *Wolford Lodge* | Pearcey Robert, *Abbey Wood* |
| Spark Samuel, maltster, *Abbey Mills* | Saunders Henry ‖ Smith Robert |
| Stuart Henry, blacksmith | Spark Peter ‖ Spark Samuel |
| Squire Ann, schoolmistress | Tucker Wm. ‖ White Henry |
| Willie Edward, beerseller | White Henry, *Wolford* |
| | Wood John, *Halshay* |

*William White's* History gazetteer and directory of Devonshire *(1850)* was the first to include entries for every parish in the county. This full coverage was continued for Devon by various publishers, notably Kelly, until 1939.

hundreds. After an introduction giving such details as the location of the community, its administrative structure, major buildings, public institutions and statistical information, there are alphabetical or sometimes classified lists of traders and frequently a separate list of the major private residents. County directories usually have a general section on the county as a whole and countywide classified lists of traders similar to today's yellow pages. Town directories frequently have listings arranged by street starting with Exeter and Plymouth in the 1870s.

Not all inhabitants are listed. Typically there is one entry for every ten inhabitants in smaller settlements and a lower proportion in larger towns. These lists concentrate on employers or self-employed traders. Entries are not always regularly updated and instances of plagiarism are not unknown but, given the immense task of collecting data, directories generally provide a remarkably full picture of the community in the past.

In Devon good sets of directories are to be found in the major local studies collections in Exeter, Plymouth, Torquay and Barnstaple. Record Offices also have collections as do non-public libraries such as the Devon and Exeter Institution. Branch libraries and museums frequently have examples of county or local directories and photocopied extracts from the county directories for the period 1822-1939 are included in the parish packs which can be found in most branch libraries and schools in Devon. In the larger libraries directories are sometimes only available on microfiches because of their fragility. The larger libraries also have back runs of telephone directories which pick up after the trade directories cease publication. A list of directory holdings in major Devon libraries has been produced by Devon Library Services.

Directories are easily approachable sources for most levels of student and can be used to trace the changing pattern of trades in a community, to check continuity of ownership (e.g. of farms or businesses), the distribution of family names etc. They are of some use for property history where properties are named or numbered. Students could attempt to compile a present-day directory of their area and draw conclusions on such matters as the relative levels of self-sufficiency of the local community.

Further reading:

Norton, Jane E. *A guide to the national and provincial directories of England and Wales, excluding London, published before 1856.* (Rev ed, 1984).

Shaw, Gareth and Tipper, Alison. *British directories: a bibliography and guide to directories published in England and Wales (1850-1950) and Scotland (1773-1950)* (1988)

Shaw, Gareth. *British directories as sources in historical geography* (1982).

Shaw, Gareth 'Directories and the local historian: ii. Methods of compilation and the work of large-scale publishers', *Local history magazine*, 45 (July/Aug 1994), 10-14.

### 3.15. NEWSPAPERS

The first provincial newspaper in Devon was published in about 1704 although early copies have completely disappeared. Since that date more than 250 different newspapers have appeared with over 350 different changes of name. Files of local newspapers are held in the main local studies libraries and in several museums in Devon. WSL has local newspaper coverage for every year from 1737 to date. Many major files have been microfilmed and to safeguard the fragile originals microfilm will always be produced where available. *The Bibliography of British newspapers: Cornwall and Devon* (British Library, 1991) provides very detailed listings of surviving newspapers in libraries throughout the world. The first Devon newspaper to be indexed was *Trewman's Exeter Flying Post*, which was indexed from 1763 to 1885 in the late 1970s. The name index ceases at 1835 but, if the field of activity is known, references to individuals can be located for the period 1836-1885. The index is held in the WSL. Other local newspapers which have been indexed since then include the *North Devon Journal* (1850-1900, Barnstaple Library), *Bideford Gazette* (Bideford Archive) and *Totnes Times* (Totnes Museum). Plymouth Local Studies Library has been selectively indexing newspapers for many years.

Until the 19th century newspapers were regularly published only in Exeter, attempts to found newspapers in Plymouth in 1718, 1759 and 1780 failing after a few years. In 1808 two newspapers were established in Plymouth but the spread was relatively slow. Barnstaple received its first newspaper in 1824, Torquay in 1839. From 1847 the spread accelerated and in 1860 the first daily newspaper was established in Plymouth. Until the early 19th century there was relatively little local

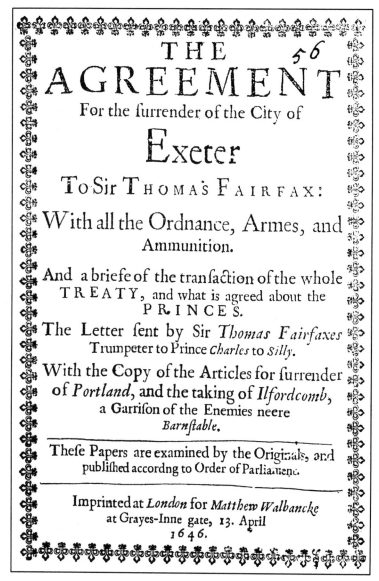

# THE 56
# AGREEMENT

For the surrender of the City of

# Exeter

To Sir THOMAS FAIRFAX:

With all the Ordnance, Armes, and Ammunition.

And a briefe of the transaction of the whole TREATY, and what is agreed about the PRINCES.

The Letter sent by Sir *Thomas Fairfaxes* Trumpeter to Prince *Charles* to *Silly*.

With the Copy of the Articles for surrender of *Portland*, and the taking of *Ilfordcomb*, a Garrison of the Enemies neere *Barnstable*.

Thefe Papers are examined by the Originals, and publifhed accordng to Order of Parliament.

Imprinted at *London* for *Matthew Walbancke* at Grayes-Inne gate, 13. April 1646.

*Newsbooks, small pamphlets, were the precursors of the newspaper. During the English Civil War they provided vital and up-to-date information on the progress of the campaigns, based on letters sent to London by eye-witnesses.*

*The masthead of Trewman's The Exeter Flying Post from 14 June, 1792. Such early papers often contained little local news. They were closely set in small type by hand and distributed by a network of newsmen on horseback. A typical circulation in the 18th century would be around 1000 copies, but each copy was read by many people.*

news and the main value of early newspapers is for advertisements. These can cover patent medicines, auctions and sales, markets, shipping, coaches and carriers. As the 19th century progressed there were frequently full reports of the meetings of local bodies which can supplement the bald accounts in official minutes. One unusual feature of early newspapers in coastal resorts such as Torquay and Ilfracombe was the regular publication during the season of a directory of local residents, services and visitors.

Further reading:
Murphy, M. *Newspapers and local history.* (1991).

### 3.151 Cuttings files
Details of these are included here as they are frequently made up largely from newspapers, but many collections contain material from a wide range of other sources including ephemera, manuscript notes, extracts from periodicals, illustrations, postcards etc. Collections are arranged in a number of ways. In WSL there are parish files with broad subject subdivisions for the smaller parishes and frequently several boxes for larger localities. The files for Exeter have a much more detailed subject subdivision. There are also separate sequences for biographical cuttings and family information. For cuttings referring to more than one place there is a sequence of subjects. The parish cuttings files in WSL have been copied for inclusion in the parish files which have been placed in

branch libraries and schools throughout the county. Other libraries maintain their cuttings collections in different ways. In Plymouth there is a classified subject sequence and Torquay place great reliance on an arrangement based on the national grid. There are special collections of cuttings in many libraries, for example the Sabina Lamb Collection, which is held in the Devon and Exeter Institution. This is much smaller than the collections in WSL but is strong on the 1950s and 1960s, a period when the WSL collection is somewhat weak.

### 3.16. PERIODICALS

A wealth of detailed information can be found in periodicals but the information is not always easy to access (see section 3.112 for periodical indexes). Among the earliest periodicals are those for learned societies such as the *Transactions of the Devonshire Association* (established 1862). Beside articles on the history of the county there are series of regular reports by sections or recorders which build up to provide detailed surveys on such topics as folklore, dialect, church plate, barrows or climate.

Question and answer periodicals began in the late nineteenth century and one of these survives today: *Devon and Cornwall notes and queries* which contains articles and reviews as well as answers to queries. County magazines appear mainly after World War II. The most familiar of these is *Devon life*. These can be useful for descriptions of houses. Publications of local history societies are also useful repositories of detailed information. *The Devon historian* is the most well-known of these. Parish and school magazines are not always passed to libraries but files can sometimes be found in local libraries, museums or deposited in record offices. There are also many specialist publications, on business, natural history etc. as well as house magazines or newsletters of various organisations. Full or partial files of many of these can be found in the main local studies libraries.

### 3.161 Monograph series

Other publications which appear in series include the *Exeter papers in economic history, Exeter studies in history* and, perhaps most important of all, the publications of the Devon and Cornwall Record Society. This body has published scholarly editions of original historical records since 1904. At first concentrating on parish registers, after 1954 the Society in its second series of publications tackled a wider range of sources including particulars of grants for monastic lands, 1536-38 (vol. 1), tax and rate assessments for Exeter (vol. 2, 22) bishops' registers 1420-1455 (vol.7, 10, 13, 16, 18), churchwardens' accounts for Ashburton 1479-1580 (vol. 15) chancery proceedings relating to shipping 1388-1493 (vol. 21), accounts of the fabric of Exeter Cathedral 1279-1353 (vol. 24, 26), household accounts 1627-59 (vol. 38, 39), and Benjamin Donn's map of Devon 1765 (vol. 9) and many other classes of records.

## 3.17. Official publications and report literature

### 3.171 Acts of Parliament

These can be among the oldest printed items of local significance, although the earliest statutes are normally available in later compilations or reprints, one of the earliest being *Statutes of the realm*, published by the Record Commission and covering statutes to 1714 - copies are in Exeter Reference Library and the University of Exeter Library. Until 1798 there were only public and private acts. In that year the category of local acts was introduced. Prior to 1798 much local legislation was therefore to be located in the public acts. A chronological list of public acts is provided by HMSO's *Chronological table of the statutes... from 1235*. This does not include local or personal acts. Sessional and later annual volumes of the public acts were published and lengthy runs of these are to be found in the University of Exeter, DRO, and the main reference libraries. Copies of many individual statutes are to be found in local studies collections.

Local and personal acts are listed in broad subject categories in HMSO's *Index to local and personal acts... 1801-1947* (1949) and the *Supplementary index to the local and personal acts... 1948-1966* (1967). Various earlier listings can be found, some including private acts. Local and personal acts are published individually, with annual or sessional indexes. Sets of annual volumes are rare; there is a set in the DRO warehouse covering 1816 to date but it is not complete. Many individual titles are held in the main local studies collections and the Record Offices also have examples, frequently with deposited plans and other documents.

Many statutes relating to Devon are listed under the heading 'Local acts' by A.A. Brockett in *The Devon Union List*. In Plymouth and Exeter listings of local acts have been compiled and a list giving locations in

Anno quinto

# Georgii II. Regis.

An Act for the better and more eafy rebuilding
of the Town of *Tiverton* in the County of
*Devon*, and for determining Differences
touching Houfes and Buildings burnt down
or demolifhed by reafon of the late dreadful fire there, and for the better preventing
Dangers from fire for the future.

WHEREAS the greateſt and Preamble.
principal Part of the Town
of Tiverton in the County of
Devon was burnt down and
deſtroyed by a ſudden and
dreadful fire, which happened
on the Fifth Day of June, One
thouſand ſeven hundred and
thirty one, occaſioned chiefly by
the great Number of thatched
Houſes and Walls in the ſaid
Town: Therefore for the bet-
ter preventing of future Damage by Fire in the
ſaid Town, May it pleaſe Your moſt Excellent Ma-
jeſty that it may be enacted, and be it enacted by
D d d d                    the

*Statutes retained an antiquated style of printing, using a gothic typeface, well
into the eighteenth century, although by 1600 this had generally been replaced
by roman type. This Act, for the rebuilding of Tiverton, was passed in 1731.*

various collections in Devon is in course of compilation. The headings used in catalogues vary, but they can normally be located under such headings as 'Statutes' or 'Great Britain. Statutes'.

### 3.172 Statutory Instruments

Also known as Statutory Rules and Orders, SIs are pieces of subsidiary legislation, issued individually, with annual cumulations which omit local items. HMSO's *Index to government orders in force* and *Table of government orders* also omits local SIs, which can be difficult to trace. An incomplete chronological set of local SIs is held in WSL and these have been indexed by subject. Many orders do not appear as SIs but are published in the *London Gazette*, lengthy files of which are held in Exeter University Library and Exeter and Plymouth Reference Libraries. There are indexes (at present quarterly but earlier annual).

### 3.173 Sessional papers

The House of Commons sessional papers, which include reports from select committees, royal commissions, surveys and returns to the House, were organised in 1801 into three groups: bills, House of Commons papers, and command papers. The first two received numbers starting a new sequence each session, command papers were numbered in longer sequences: [1-4222] 1833-69, C.1-9550 (1870-99) Cd.1-9329 (1900-18), Cmd.1-9889 (1919-56) and Cmnd.1-9927 (1956-86), Cm. 1- (1986-). Papers were published separately with indexes to enable them to be bound in volumes at the end of each session. References in indexes and footnotes frequently give the volume and page number as well as the paper number. Cumulated indexes by HMSO include the *General index... 1801-52* (3 vol), *General alphabetical index 1852-99* and the *General index 1900 to 1948/9*. For later periods there are decennial indexes. P. and G. Ford have produced lists and summaries of major parliamentary papers: *Hansard's catalogue and breviate of parliamentary papers, 1696-1834* (1953), *Select list of British parliamentary papers, 1833-1899* (Rev ed. 1970), *Breviate of parliamentary papers, 1900-1916* (1957), and the same for 1917-1939 (1951) and 1940-54 (1961) - copies can be found in the larger reference libraries and the University of Exeter Library. The easiest way to track down references in these sources is by consulting complete sets of sessional papers. These are held for the 18th century onwards in original, hard copy reprint, and microfiche in the University of Exeter. There are not as large a number of sessional publications relating specifically to the South West as there are for more industrialised areas in the 19th century. The county sections of census reports, containing statistics down to parish level, were published as sessional papers to 1921 (for enumerators' returns see section 3.353 below) and the local sections of a number of other reports can also be found in most of the main local studies libraries, for example: the Charity Commissioners (especially 1826-32 and early 20th century), the Commissioners on Municipal Corporations (1835), the reports on Boundaries of Municipal Corporations (1837), the Schools Inquiry Commission (1868), the Return of owners of land (1873), the Royal Commission on Agriculture (1895), the Prison Commissioners.

There are also sessional papers for the House of Lords, but these are largely made up of bills and are not so useful for the local historian.

### 3.174 Proceedings

The verbatim reports of the House of Commons and House of Lords which can contain debates and questions of local interest, are to be found in Exeter and Plymouth Reference collections and in the University of Exeter. Coverage of debates in both Houses is full from 1803, first by Cobbet, later by Hansard and from 1909 by Parliament itself. Debates prior to 1803 are contained in a variety of unofficial sources. The official record of proceedings are contained in the *Journals* of the House of Commons (1547-) and House of Lords (1509-). Prior to 1801 many committee reports were printed in the *Journals*. Sets of these are available in Exeter Reference and University of Exeter libraries.

### 3.175 Departmental publications

Only a small proportion of official publications are statutory or sessional publications. Those that are published by the Stationery Office are listed in the Annual lists (1920-) which have cumulated indexes. Examples of such Stationery Office publications include the local reports of the British Geological Survey and the county volumes of the census from 1931. There are also reports on economic development, especially since 1945. Among the earliest official publications that are generally available are the regional reports to the Board of Agriculture made by R.Fraser (1794), W.Marshall (1796), G.Vancouver (1808) and others (see section 4.44 below).

From 1980 non Stationery Office publications are listed by Chadwyck-Healey in the *Catalogue of British official publications not published by*

# REPORT OF THE COMMISSIONERS

## *FOR INQUIRING CONCERNING,*

## CHARITIES.

## COUNTY OF DEVON.

## HUNDRED OF BAMPTON.

### BAMPTON.

#### SIR JOHN ACLAND'S GIFT.

Sir *John Acland*, Baronet, in 1619, by the same deed poll by which he gave 52*s.* a year to be weekly distributed in bread, amongst the poor of the borough of Tiverton, and 26*s.* per annum to be distributed also in bread amongst the poor of the parish of Halberton, (as is stated in the reports on those parishes,) gave in like manner 26*s.* a year, to be paid by the mayor, recorder, and the two most ancient aldermen of the city of Exeter for the time being, to the churchwardens for the time being of the parish of Bampton, for the buying and providing weekly for ever, of six penny loaves and a half of wheaten bread, to be distributed every Sabbath day immediately after morning prayer, unto seven such of the poorest sort of people of the parish of Bampton, as the minister, constable, churchwardens and overseers for the poor of the said parish for the time being, or the more part of them should think fit and appoint.

The sum of 1*l.* 6*s.* is paid yearly by the chamber of Exeter to the vicar of the parish and is laid out in bread, which is by him distributed annually on some Sunday in November, to as many poor persons as the bread will supply. In respect of the period of giving away the bread, the directions of the donor are departed from, and we see no reason why the weekly distribution he has prescribed should not be effected.

#### JOHN TRISTRAM'S GIFT.

*John Tristram*, by will dated 16th May 1628, gave to the most impotent and poorest people of the town and parish of Bampton 40*s.* yearly, to be payable to the collectors for the poor out of a parcel of land, situate in Bampton, called Little Pilemore, with a power of distress in case the annuity should be unpaid, and he directed that the annuity should be distributed unto the said poor yearly.

The estate called Little Pilemore, belongs to John Nicholas Fazakerly, Esq. it forms a part of Duvall Farm, in the parish of Bampton. The annuity of 1*l.* 16*s.* (4*s.* having been deducted in modern times as it is supposed for land-tax,) has been paid regularly up to Christmas 1818, to the overseers of the poor, and by them distributed after a vestry meeting at Christmas to the poor of the parish, in small sums of 1*s.* 6*d.* each. From 1719 to 1737 the whole annuity was paid without deduction.

#### ROBERT MOGRIDGE'S GIFT.

From an extract from the will of *Robert Mogridge*, which is stated to have been dated the year 1645, it appears that he gave to the poor of Bampton 5*l.* yearly, for ever, and 20*s.* yearly for ever, to the churchwardens of that parish, such annuities to be paid to the churchwardens yearly, on the 1st of March, out of the profits of his land in Hill Bishops, and he directed that no person or family should have less than 5*s.* or more than 10*s.* in the distribution; that such of the poor as had no part one year should have part in the next if they should be found worthy; that the distribution should be made on the 29th or 30th of March yearly, amongst the most honest and religious poor people, and that if any of his

A

*Reports of the Charity Commissioners were among the most important of early Government publications. This edition was published 1826-30.*

*HMSO.* Prior to that date it is often necessary to search in departmental publication lists as not all such publications appear in the *British national bibliography.* Recent examples of departmental publications which include titles of local interest are the reports of HM inspectors of schools, published by the Department of Education and Science, Home Office publications, such as those of HM inspectors of constabulary, and the publications of the Transport and Road Research Laboratory.

The main local studies collections attempt to collect such Stationery Office and departmental publications as they can identify, but much is missed. They can be located in catalogues under the name of the department or committee (sometimes as a subdivision of the heading 'Great Britain') or under the name of the compiler or chairman. In cases where authorship is unclear the item may be located under title. The parish packs found in most branches and schools normally include local extracts from the census reports and the Charity Commissioners.

Further reading: Pemberton, J.E. *British official publications* (2 ed, 1973)

### 3.176 Local government publications
From the 19th century the minutes of local authorities began to be circulated in print. These contain a wealth of detail, down to permissions for the development of individual properties but they are complex documents to work through as several committees could deal with the same matter and they are normally unindexed. The reports of individual officers and departments, such as the medical officer of health were also published, often with financial and statistical tables. The *Analysis of survey for the Devon County Development Plan* appeared in 1952 and the *Report of survey for the Structure Plan* in 1977 and each have been followed by an ever increasing flood of planning documentation, much of it containing valuable surveys of the social and economic conditions in the county. Local plans have been produced more recently by district councils and there have been separate plans for Dartmoor National Park since 1977. Publications on specific topics include annual reviews on tourism, mineral working, conservation, employment, transport policies and various other subjects.

Further reading:
Devon County Council. *Planning in Devon: an information handbook* (updated at intervals)

### 3.177. Report literature

Besides local councils, a wide range of bodies produce reports, known as 'grey literature' because it is difficult to track down. Producers include health authorities, the public utilities, commercial companies and academic institutions. Some information can only be found in such reports, which often receive limited circulation or are expensive to acquire. For example South West Water produced a wide range of information on climate in the 1970s. Since the 1960s the regional surveys of the Agricultural Economics Unit at the University of Exeter include a wealth of statistical and economic data for the historian of agriculture.

### 3.18. PRINTED EPHEMERA

Only a sample of the wealth of ephemeral printed material can be collected. Posters, brochures, timetables, theatre programmes and other flimsy items are not intended for preservation but, where they survive they are frequently attractive items and give a vivid insight into everyday life. Libraries, museums and record office all have material of this type. Some material, such as the execution broadsheets, which survive in an unusual number for Exeter in the 18th century are flimsy, others such as estate sale particulars, can be quite substantial publications, often with detailed plans and illustrations of the properties to be sold. See section 3.37 for further details on sale particulars.

## 3.2 VISUAL SOURCES

There are few visual materials for Devon before the 18th century and then only the major historical sites are recorded. Only the arrival of the camera made everyday life the subject of illustrations and there is no certainty of finding a large-scale plan of any parish before the tithe survey of about 1840 (see 3.224 below).

### 3.21 ILLUSTRATIONS

Illustrations can convey information in a way that is impossible in written form but, for that very reason they pose problems in indexing, storage and access. There are large collections of illustrative material in Devon, but it is not always easy to identify the precise image required and it is advisable for researchers to make prior enquiry that there will be material available. The main collections are held by the larger libraries but many extensive collections of local scenes can be found in museums. Generally museums are better at indexing artists than are libraries, which are more interested in the topographical content of the items.

There are sometimes negatives available for illustrations and where this is the case it can considerably cut the costs of making photographic copies. In many collections photographic copies or digital scans have to be made through a designated photographer and photography by users may not be permitted. A royalty may also be payable should illustrations from collections be used in publications or broadcasts.

### 3.211 Photographs

A useful recent book on the use of photographs for historical research is G.A. Oliver's *Photographs and local history* (1989). Other titles are *Recording the past: a photographer's handbook* by Eric Houlder (1988) and *Dating old photographs* by Robert Pols (1992). There has been a considerable growth of books of early photographs since the 1960s and there are few areas of the county which have not been covered. If reference for the purposes of private study is required it may often be most convenient for such volumes to be consulted before the collections in the local studies collections are approached. Such volumes are normally shelved with the histories and guidebooks of the locality in question and loan copies of many titles are available. A national example is the *Britain in old photographs series*, published by Alan Sutton. Local publishers such as Obelisk in Exeter and A.L. Clamp in Plymouth issue many titles made up largely of old photographs which have frequently been made available by private individuals. These often have the advantage of having been carefully identified by the owners.

The Francis Frith Collection is a nationwide collection built up by a leading commercial photographer over the period 1860-1970. The entire collection for the British Isles has been made available on microfiche and the Devon section, containing some 15 349 illustrations, is available in WSL and North Devon Athenaeum. A further set has been split between the main local studies collections in Plymouth, Torquay and Exmouth. A place listing is available. The original glass negatives are deposited in Birmingham Central Library and fine quality copies can be purchased. Many Francis Frith photographs are included in general illustrations and postcard collections. They can frequently be identified by the letters FF preceding the negative number. Another early photographer active in Devon was Francis Bedford and some examples of his albums of photographs, some dating from the 1860s, can be found in the main collections.

There have been a number of photographic surveys, often carried out by Manpower Services Commission projects, although one of the earliest, the Exeter Pictorial Record Society, held in WSL, dates from the period 1900-1914. The items (which include prints and drawings) have been rephotographed. There is no current countywide photographic survey being undertaken. The historic photographs collected by the Beaford Community Archive have been deposited in the North DRO together with listings and the views of North Devon by the contemporary photographer James Ravilious which will be made available there once indexing is complete. The Dartington Rural Archive has performed a similar function for the south of Devon and there are collections of photographs in many museums across the county. The photographic archive of the *Western morning news* has been deposited in the Record Office in Plymouth, but much work has to be undertaken on conservation of the glass plates and their indexing.

Picture postcards, which originated in the 1890s and were especially popular during the period up to 1914, are held by some local studies collections but are not always housed separately from the main illustrations collections. The arrangement is usually by place.

Lantern slides have been collected by libraries but, because of their fragility, they will only be produced for serious researchers when no alternative is available.

Further reading:
Miller, S.T. 'The value of photographs as historical evidence', *Local historian* 15:8, Nov 1984, 468-473.
Scott, C.G. *Photographers in Devon 1842-1939: a brief directory*, Royal Photographic Society, 1994

### 3.212 Prints
Over 3500 engravings and lithographs of Devon scenes are listed in J.V.Somers Cocks *Devon topographical prints, 1660-1870: a topographical guide* (1977) which also has an excellent introduction outlining the history of topographical prints in Devon, as well as a list of sources in

which series of prints are to be found. Many collections in Devon have used this catalogue as a basis for arranging their own collections of prints and it is always worth while quoting the catalogue numbers of items you wish to see. Copies of the catalogue are available in many libraries. Certain categories of material, such as wood engravings and interiors are for the most part omitted. There are indexes of artists and engravers and a very selective subject index.

### 3.213. Drawings
There are collections of drawings in most local studies collections but those of artistic merit are more likely to be found in museums. This is reflected in the standard directory: *A guide to British topographical collections* by M.Barley (1974). Not all collections house original works of art separately from other prints and photographs and there are not always full indexes of artists and subjects.

### 3.214. Portraits
Portraits are usually filed alphabetically by the name of the subject and there are collections of varying sizes in many of the larger local studies collections. Only the most important personages had their portraits painted or engraved but early photographs of many individuals can be found in the form of cabinet photographs on cards with details of the photographer on the verso. Since individual's names are not normally identified, these are frequently to be found in the costume section of the illustrations collection.

### 3.215 Aerial photographs
These can be found in most of the larger collections, not always separately filed from the main photograph sequences. Beside their value for tracing the development of communities, they are invaluable for showing crop-marks which reveal otherwise hidden prehistoric sites. For this reason one of the main collections in the county is held by the Sites and Monuments Register at County Hall, Exeter. A guide to collections is given by W. Minchinton in 'Air photographs for the Devon historian' in *Devon Historian* 16 pp25-26. A more recent guide, with notes on their use for teaching is: Devon Education's *A Devon approach to geography in the national curriculum: finding and using aerial photographs* (1991). A useful collection of aerial views of archaeological sites is *Devon's past: an aerial view* by Frances Griffiths (1988).

*Before the development of photography engravings were the main method of providing multiple copies of illustrations. It was possible to re-engrave plates to incorporate changes. This view of Exeter Cathedral (Somers Cocks catalogue no. 841) first appeared in 1853 but was amended after the rebuilding of St Mary Major between 1865 and 1867. The figures in the foreground have not changed their position in the intervening years.*

**3**

## 3.22. MAPS

Extensive collections of maps in hard copy and microfilm can be found in the main local studies libraries. Museums and record offices also hold maps, as does the Department of Geography at the University of Exeter.

### 3.221. Early maps

The tradition of surveying was not so well developed in earlier centuries in this country as on the continent and much reliance was placed on written description of estates until the eighteenth century. Most local studies libraries only hold a small selection of the earliest engraved county maps whose interest is decorative rather than topographical, but WSL has examples of virtually every county map produced between the first survey of Devon, made by Christopher Saxton in the 1570s, until the mid 19th century through its acquisition of the Batten and Bennett Collection in 1997. There are also early estate plans in the Record Office. Until Benjamin Donn's prize-winning survey of 1765 almost all Devon maps derived from Saxton's survey. Donn only showed the main roads. Side roads and tracks were first shown by the Ordnance Survey in 1809 and fields by the tithe maps of about 1840 (held in record offices) and the 1:2500 Ordnance Survey plans from the 1860s (held in larger libraries).

Apart from the Ordnance Survey, two cartographers have produced one inch to the mile maps of Devon: Benjamin Donn whose *Map of the county of Devon* was published in 1765 (reprinted by the Devon and Cornwall Record Society in 1965) and C. and J.Greenwood's *Map of the county of Devon* from an actual survey made in the years 1825 & 1826 (1827). Both are widely available in the major local studies collections. The standard source for Devon's early county maps is: *The printed maps of Devon 1575-1837*, by K. Batten and F. Bennett (1996).

### 3.222. Ordnance Survey

The establishment of the Ordnance Survey in 1791 brought a new standard of mapping to the British Isles. Photographs of the manuscript drafts used for the first edition of the Ordnance Survey one inch to a mile map of Devon are held in WSL. These were produced at scales ranging from two- to six inches to one mile between 1784 and 1809 and the originals are in the British Library. Although field boundaries are shown, these are normally schematic only. J.B. Harley of Exeter

42

University has written two guides to OS maps: *The historian's guide to Ordnance Survey maps* (1964) and *Ordnance Survey maps: a descriptive manual* (1975). R. Oliver's *Ordnance Survey maps: a guide for historians* (1994) is a revision of Harley's work.

The first edition (Old Series) of the one-inch-to-a-mile map covering Devon was published in 1809. The same plates were used until the 1880s with selective alteration for railways, new roads and other major changes. The facsimile published by Harry Margary in book form uses the earliest version of the plates while the sheets published by David & Charles are taken from late electrotype plates, usually of the 1870s and 1880s and show railways. Both have extensive documentation by J.B. Harley.

The second edition (New Series) was current in Devon from about 1886 to 1910, the third edition from about 1910 to 1918 the fourth edition (Popular Edition) from about 1918 to 1933, the fifth edition from about 1933 to 1939, the sixth edition (New Popular) from about 1946 to 1957, and the seventh series from about 1953 to 1972), at which date they were replaced by the 1:50 000 first series (1974-). The second (Landranger) series was introduced in Devon in *c.* 1985. While too small for detailed local history research, these small scales were revised more frequently than the larger scales and can record major changes. Useful guides by R. Oliver are his *Guide to Ordnance Survey one inch seventh series* (3rd ed, 1990), and his *Guide to the Ordnance Survey one inch new popular edition* (2nd ed, 1989).

The large-scale survey of the British Isles was delayed by a dispute over the scale at which it was to be published and it did not commence publication in Devon until 1864. From this period the first edition of the six-inch-to-a-mile (1:10 560) and 1:2500 plans of the Plymouth and Torbay areas were published concurrently. Coverage of the remainder of the county had to wait until 1885-90. A second edition was published for most of the county in 1905-6 and revisions for the built-up areas also appeared, mostly in the 1930s. The central areas of Dartmoor and Exmoor were not covered at a scale of 1:2500. Devon was covered by 139 sheets, numbered in strips across the county from west to east and north to south. The 1:10 560 maps appeared in four sub-sheets (NW NE SW and SE), the 1:2500 in 16 subsheets, numbered from 1 to 16. The Ordnance Survey's key sheets have recently been reprinted:

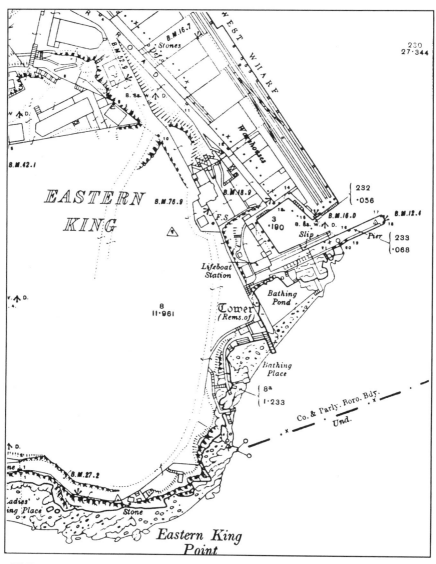

All Devon, except for the centre of Dartmoor has been surveyed at a scale of 1: 2500. This extract is from sheet 123.11, covering Plymouth and dating from 1914. Despite the high level of detail - individual properties are shown and even the layout of the railway track at Great Western Dock - the sensitive military site at Eastern King has not been surveyed.

*Indexes to the 1:2500 and six inch scale maps: England and Wales.* The major local studies collections have the first and second edition 1:2500 and 1:10 560 sheets for their own area in aperture card or microfiche. Revised editions must be consulted in hard copy. Between 1855 and 1892 the Ordnance Survey published even larger scale plans (typically 1:500) of the following towns in Devon: Barnstaple, Bideford, Brixham, Crediton, Dartmouth, Dawlish, Exeter, Exmouth, Ilfracombe, Newton Abbot, Plymouth, Tavistock, Teignmouth, Tiverton, Torquay and Totnes. Microfiches of these extremely detailed plans are available in the appropriate area local studies collections with a full set for the county in WSL. Access is through a combination of listings and key sheets. Parish packs in branch libraries and schools should contain copies of the second edition Ordnance Survey 1:10 560 local sheet.

From 1945 large-scale Ordnance Survey plans were based on a metric national grid. The 100 Km squares which cover Devon are SS, ST SX and SY. Within these main squares references are given by counting first the eastings and then the northings. Thus a two figure reference (e.g. ST12 is accurate to within ten kilometers, a four figure reference (e.g. ST1234) to within one kilometer and a six-figure reference (e.g. ST123456) to within one hundred meters. The national grid maps have been published at the following scales since 1945:

1:25 000: sheets cover one 10km square (e.g. ST10) or two adjacent 10km squares (e.g. ST10/20). The series is currently published in the 20x10km format and is known as the Pathfinder series, the sheets also receiving sequential numbering covering the whole country. Maps wholly within the area covered by Outdoor Leisure or Explorer maps are not normally separately updated. Public libraries in Devon hold the following areas:

> WSL: Devon, Cornwall, Somerset, Dorset
> Plymouth: Devon, Cornwall
> Torquay: Devon, Cornwall
> Barnstaple: Devon, North Cornwall, West Somerset.

1:10 560 (from c.1970 1:10,000). Sheets cover one 5km square (e.g. ST10NW, ST10NE, ST10SW, ST10SE). Public library holdings in Devon are as follows:
> WSL: Devon, Cornwall, Dorset, Somerset

Plymouth: Devon, Cornwall
Torquay: South Devon
Barnstaple: North Devon

1:2500. Sheets cover a 1km square (e.g. ST1234) or two adjacent squares (e.g. ST1234/1334). Where 1:1250 plans are published this scale was discontinued and the centres of Dartmoor and Exmoor were never covered at this scale. Public library holdings are:

WSL: East Devon area and 15km radius of Exeter
Plymouth: West Devon area
Torquay: South Devon area
Barnstaple: North Devon area
Exmouth: Exmouth area only

SUSI (unpublished interim updates) were not normally acquired by libraries. In 1992 the publication of plans at the scales of 1:2500 and 1:1250 was discontinued and succeeded by Superplan, a system of computerised updating. In view of the expense, print-outs from these sheets are not normally acquired by Devon Library Services but it is possible to consult large-scale mapping of the entire county on computer at WSL and Barnstaple, and to obtain A4 print-outs under the fair dealing clause of the Copyright Act.

1:1250. Sheets cover an area 500 meters square (e.g. SX9292NW, SX9292NE, SX9292SW, SX9292SE. Only the major towns are covered. Public library holdings: as for 1:2500 sheets.

### 3.223. Town plans
There are few large-scale town plans before 1800, and most recent ones are derived from Ordnance Survey mapping. A great problem is that many publishers did not add dates of publication to town plans. Folded town plans held by the main local studies collections are usually filed alphabetically by place but are also frequently found in local guidebooks.

### 3.224. Thematic maps
TITHE MAPS AND APPORTIONMENTS
Mostly dating from about 1840 these are deposited in DRO which also holds estate and other plans. The schedules list farms and other premis-

es with names of owners and occupiers, sometimes including the land use, and give valuation. Tithe surveys, often the earliest large-scale surveys of parishes, are invaluable for tracing estates of the major landowners. They also show roads and watercourses. Enclosure Acts with the accompanying surveys are relatively uncommon in Devon and largely confined to the east of the county.

GEOLOGICAL SURVEY

Sheet numbering is based on the 2nd series 1:63 360 of the Ordnance Survey but sheets are now being reissued on the scale of 1:50 000. For many sheets there is a geological memoir which includes sections on economic geology. Area collections hold local sheets with regional coverage in WSL.

LAND UTILISATION SURVEY

Produced at a scale of 1:63 360, mainly in the 1940s and not updated. Revised sheets are kept at Bedford College in the University of London. WSL holds the sheets for Devon.

LAND USE MAPS

Only a very few sheets have been issued at a scale of 1:25 000. These are held in WSL and other major collections.

AGRICULTURAL LAND CLASSIFICATION

Published in the 1970s on the sheet lines of the seventh edition of the 1:63 360. For some sheets there is a brief accompanying memoir. There is also a 1:250 000 sheet for the whole region. Sets for Devon are held in the larger local studies collections.

SOIL SURVEY

Not all of the county has been covered at a large scale. For large-scale sheets that have been issued (some at 1:25 000, some at 1:63 360) there is normally also a memoir. Sheets and memoirs are held in the larger local studies collections.

GOAD PLANS

The shopping centre surveys are compiled for the larger towns and are updated annually or every two years. In the 1970s they succeeded the Goad insurance plans which had been published for Exeter and Plymouth only in Devon between 1888 and 1962 at a scale of 1 inch to

40 feet. These were updated by means of paste-on slips and are extremely detailed, showing the fabric of individual buildings and the location of fire hydrants. They are available in Plymouth Local Studies Library and WSL on aperture cards.

NAVIGATION CHARTS
Besides those published by the Admiralty Hydrographic Department, the firm of Imray have published charts for yachtsmen. Sheets for local waters are held in local studies collections. It should be noted that the Admiralty do not allow any copying from charts which are still in copyright.

FINDING AIDS
There is no comprehensive published list of maps covering Devon. Library finding aids are a mixture of print-outs from a computer database (as in WSL), marked up key sheets or card listings.

Further reading:
Hindle, B.P. *Maps for local history* (1988).
Kain, R.J.P. *The tithe maps of England and Wales.* (1995).
Smith, D. *Maps and plans for the local historian and collector* (1988).

**3.23.** AUDIO-VISUAL RESOURCES
The most important repository in Devon for film and video is the TSW Film and Television Archive in Plymouth which is based on the extensive film collections of Television South West and its predecessor Westward Television. Despite discussions at various times, there is no central oral history collection in Devon, but various projects have been collecting oral history as well as folk music. Section six of *Local studies in Devon: a guide to resources* gives details of a number of these but it should be noted that many have limited access and listening facilities for the public.

## 3.3. ARCHIVES AND RECORDS

Archival and official documents should normally be located in record offices. Researchers should ensure that they have checked published and secondary sources before consulting original records. In many cases there may be published transcripts available or the information may already have been extracted in a published book or periodical article. DRO issues a *Guide to sources* which includes 'Lists and indexes: a brief guide' as well as notes on sources on such subjects as family history, house history, farming history, transport history, martime history and crime and punishment. There are also guides to specific categories of records. *HMSO Sectional list 17* covers the publications of the Royal Commission on Historical Manuscripts, the body which maintains the National Register of Archives in London. This incorporates information supplied by national and local record offices across the country and also houses the Manorial Documents register. The database of the National Register of Archives can now be accessed on the Internet at http://www.hmc.gov.uk and can give references to many stray records relating to Devon.

### 3.31 PARISH RECORDS

The contents of the parish chest is one of the first ports of call for the historian who is conducting in-depth research into the history of a parish. Of the items it contains the best-known are the parish registers.

### 3.311. Parish Registers

Parish registers were introduced in 1538 and until the advent of civil registration in 1837 provide the main source for tracing baptisms (not births), marriages and burials (not deaths). Some of the earliest registers were kept on loose sheets of paper and relatively few survive in Devon but a canon of 1597 required their copying retrospectively into parchment books and the making of annual transcripts of entries for the Diocese. The production of Bishops' Transcripts in Devon was largely ignored and few start earlier than 1606, but in many instances the series, which have always formed part of the diocesan records, fill gaps where the original parish copies have disappeared. The Civil War and Commonwealth interrupted the production of parish registers with Bishops' Transcripts ceasing for twenty years from 1642 although in 1653 a layman, confusingly known as the Parish Register, was appointed in each parish to maintain registration. Even after the Restoration there are many gaps in Bishops' Transcripts until the 1720s. From 1754 Lord Hardwicke's marriage act introduced printed books of forms and the parties and witnesses had to sign or give their marks - important evidence for literacy. In 1812 the Parochial Registers Act introduced printed forms for baptisms which included the names, residences and occupations of the parents, and for burials which included the residence and age at death. From the introduction of Civil

Coplestone, Ann, d. of Mr Anthony & Betty Cople-
stone ... ... ... born 24 July 28 Dec.
Coleridge, Samuel Taylor,[1] s. of John & Ann
Coleridge, the Vicar, born 21 October last about
11 o'clock in the forenoon ... ... ... 30 Dec.
Coles, William, s. of John & Sarah Coles ... 30 Dec.
Clark, Tryphena, d. of Joseph & Mary Clark ... 30 Dec.
Berry, Thomas, s. of Mary Berry [illeg.] privately
bap. ... ... ... ... ... 30 Dec.
1773. Mitchell, John, s. of William & Jane Mitchell ... 1 Jan.
Stafford, Elizabeth, d. of Richard & Elizabeth
Stafford ... ' ... ... ... 1 Jan.
Davies, Charles, s. of Ann Davies [illeg.], Peter
Branscomb being reputed father, aged about 22
weeks ... ... ... ... ... 2 Jan.
Bond, Elizabeth, d. of Thomas & Ann Bond, being
3 years old the 20th day of last July, in 1772 ... 2 Jan.
Blackmore, Charles, s. of Joseph & Jane Blackmore,
of Tipton ... ... ... ... 10 Jan.
Cocks, William, s. of John & Sarah Cocks ... 13 Jan.
Riggs, Thomas, s. of Thomas & Jane Riggs,
privately bap. ... ... ... ... 13 Jan.
  [1] The poet.

*Introduced in 1538, parish registers record baptisms, mariages and burials in
each parish. This extract is from the parish register of Ottery St Mary and
includes the entry for the baptism of the poet Samuel Taylor Coleridge. Also
shown is the transcript published by the Devon & Cornwall Record Society
between 1908 and 1929.*

Registration in 1837 the marriage register was changed to include the ages of the parties, their occupations and their fathers' names and occupations. A good introduction to Anglican and other registers is given by Hugh Peskett in *Guide to the parish and non-parochial registers of Devon and Cornwall 1538-1837* (Devon and Cornwall Record Society, 1979). Since this work was compiled virtually all Devon parish registers have been called into the three record offices in Devon under the Parochial Records Measure of 1978 and a better guide to location is now the DRO's *Parish, non-parochial and civil registers in the DRO* (regularly updated). The current registers (which may in smaller parishes extend back a considerable time) remain with the church.

While most parish registers and diocesan transcripts are therefore available, normally on microfiche, in the Devon's record offices and service points, other transcripts and indexes are also to be found. The Devon and Cornwall Record Society has transcribed and published a number of registers, including notably Colyton, which has been used for a range of important demographic studies. These published transcripts are widely available in libraries. The Society's library, available to members in WSL, includes several hundred additional unpublished parish register transcripts and also includes Boyd's and Fursdon's marriage indexes and an index to marriage licences, all typescripts or manuscripts. Baptisms and marriages, but not burials, for parishes held in the Society's collection along with some other parishes have been indexed by the Mormons and are available on microfiche as the *International Genealogical Index*. Various versions of the Devon section of this Index are available in libraries throughout Devon. It is available on CD-ROM under the name *Family Search* in the Mormon Library in Plymouth. The Devon Family History Society is involved in indexing Devon marriages from 1813-1837 and will extend coverage back to 1754. They have also indexed burials in many Devon parishes, normally from 1812-1837. The growth of nonconformity means that coverage becomes increasingly patchy in Devon, although the established church was frequently used by dissenters for baptism, marriage and burial, and certainly during the period of Civil Registration the registry office indexes are the most comprehensive source for births, marriage and deaths.

### 3.312. Other parish records
These are normally to be found in record offices. Unlike parish registers these for the most part have not been transcribed indexed or published.

**3**

Stuart Raymond's *Devon: a genealogical bibliography* lists examples of many parish records which have been the subject of books or periodical articles relating to specific localities.

Since Tudor times the parish has had a wide range of administrative activities and has generated a variety of records. From 1555, for example, each parish was made responsible for its highways and a series of Acts culminating in those of 1597 and 1601 obliged them to relieve the poor.

Vestry minutes contain the main proceedings of the parish and give an account of the vestry's activities in a wide range of areas.

Churchwarden's accounts in a few instances pre-date parish registers and several have been transcribed and published. Examples include Ashburton (1479-1580), Chagford (1480-1600), Hartland (1597-1706) and Morebath (1520-1573). They note expenditure on a remarkably wide range of matters from road repairs to the payment of bounty for killing vermin.

Rating lists indicate the liability of each named person, but only rarely give the names of properties on which their liability was assessed. There may be separate rating assessments for poor rates, church rates and highway rates. See the Historical Association's *Short guide to records: rate books* (1994).

The accounts of the Overseer of the Poor are perhaps the most informative for social historians. The parish was responsible for poverty relief until the Poor Law Reform Act of 1834 set up poor law unions (see 3.341 below). Among the records of most value for family historians are the apprenticeship papers, although these do not survive for all parishes. Poor law apprenticeships were normally for menial rather than skilled employments, such as domestic service or agricultural labour. Those for Stockleigh English are discussed in the *Transactions of the Devonshire Association* (1901) p.484-94. Settlement papers are useful for studying migration. Other papers which may survive are bastardy records, vagrant searches, removal orders and workhouse accounts. A listing of these groups of records is given by the DRO in *Parish poor law records in Devon* (1993)

Records of parish charities, often including charity schools, can provide valuable information on the way public services were provided as a result of private philanthropy. Information is often summaried in the reports of the Charity Commissioners (see section 3.173).

Civil parishes were established in 1894 and many of their records are also deposited in the DRO. In a few cases copies of minutes may also be found in the local library or museum.

Further reading:
Tate, W.E. *The parish chest.* (3rd ed, 1983)
West, J. *Village records.* (Rev. ed, 1997)
Cole, A. *An introduction to poor law documents before 1834.* (1993).

## 3.32 COUNTY RECORDS

### 3.321 Quarter sessions
While starting as a court of law in Tudor times for less serious crimes than the Assizes, the Quarter Sessions had many administrative functions attached to it over the centuries. Records of a wide range of activities are held in the DRO. Beside the County Quarter Sessions there were also separate sessions for Exeter, Plymouth, Bideford, South Molton, Dartmouth, Tiverton and Torrington. The main records of the Court in session, the order books, extend from 1592 to 1971 for Devon, while rolls and books cover Exeter from 1557 to 1971.

Other records include gaol calendars and records of transportation (for Devon from 1718 to 1775). Deeds of bargain and sale were enrolled from 1536. Plans of major statutory undertakings, such as roads, bridges, ferries, harbours and railways were deposited pursuant to a House of Commons order of 1792, though most for Devon do not survive until after 1810. The Sessions were charged with maintaining registers of various kinds. Among those which survive are registers for freemasons' lodges and printing presses. Publicans' recognizances are a useful source for those studying the history of inns, although the name of the inn is not always given.

### 3.322 County Council records
Devon County Council was established, like all other county councils in 1889 and took over most of the adminstrative work of the quarter

sessions. At first they had relatively few powers but from the start the records of the County Treasurer survive in the DRO. The gradual growth of the county's administrative activities is seen by the Record Office's holdings of other series of records, for example those for education (from 1890), roads and bridges (from 1892), smallholdings (from 1910), public health (from 1912), public assistance (from 1929), planning (from 1931). Many of these functions, for example health, have now been transferred to other authorities. Council minutes were printed and made more widely available from 1905.

Further reading:
Emmison, F.G. and Gray, I. *County records.* (New ed, 1987).
Devon Record Office. *Assizes and quarter sessions in Exeter.* (1971).

### 3.33 MUNICIPAL RECORDS

For the smaller towns these may differ little from parish records. In some instance the trustees of an influential charitable institution may have taken over a variety of functions. One Devon example is the feofees of Colyton. Larger incorporated boroughs would have a council with a mayor or portreeve, aldermen, councillors and one or more paid officials. The basis of the early powers would be laid down, confirmed or amended in a series of charters. The meetings of the council and its various committees would be recorded in minute books. Details of financial management will appear in the account books of the Chamberlain or a similar official. Some towns had powers to hold petty sessions or even quarter sessions. Rating records, often arranged by street, can be a useful guide to the development of the town. Some towns also maintained registers of freemen who had the right to trade and to bind apprentices. This structure of economic control became less strict during the 18th century but freedom records are a useful guide to trades before the development of directories. The Municipal Corporations Act of 1835 brought the old and sometimes corrupt and oligarchic corporations into line. Gradually separate committees began to oversee special functions. The records of the Exeter Watch Committee for example start in 1836. The City of Exeter has one of the finest collections of archives of any provincial town in England and there is no space to deal with them in any detail here. A published listing of the Exeter records with extensive extracts is given in the Historical Manuscripts Commission's rather confusingly arranged *Report on the Records of the City of Exeter* (HMSO, 1916). During the 19th century several towns had Improvement Commissioners which stood apart from the original corporation.

Further reading:
West, J. *Town records*. (1983).

### 3.341 Poor law unions.
These date from the late 1830s and early 1840s when groups of parishes were combined into poor law unions after the Poor Law Reform Act of 1834. The account and minute books contain data on the cost of poor relief, workhouse rules and administrations, schooling and discipline. Unions were also responsible for providing medical care at parish level.

Further reading:
Gibson, J. *Poor law union records. 3: South West England, the Marches and Wales* (1993).
Historial Association. *Short guides to records: guardian's minute books* (1994)

### 3.342 School boards.
The most important records are school log books, compiled from 1863 on instruction from the Board of Education. Admission registers survive in Devon from the 1850s when many National and British Schools were built. The 1870 Education Act ordered the setting up of local school boards and records from 1871, including plans, survive in the DRO.

### 3.343 Health authorities, hospitals.
Local boards of health were set up after surveys in the mid-nineteenth century. Many of the annual reports of the medical officers of health were printed and so can be found in libraries as well as record offices. The University of Exeter is conducting a project to locate historical medical records in the region.

### 3.344 Turnpike trusts.
These were set up in Devon from the 1750s and were private bodies maintaining stretches of highway between the main towns. Not all

records survive, but a number can be found in the Record Office. Records also had to be deposited with the Quarter Sessions. From 1864 much of the work of the turnpike trusts was taken over by highway boards.

### 3.345 Fishery boards.
These were set up in the 19th and 20th centuries. Those for the Taw and Torridge, Exe, Teign, Axe and Dart survive in the DRO.

### 3.346 Coroners.
These are public records but few survive in Devon. There is very limited access to more recent records.

### 3.347 Petty sessions
These dealt with lesser crimes such as poaching and minor theft. Judicial records survive from the 19th century only.

### 3.348 Electoral records.
Electoral registers have been compiled since the 1832 Reform Act and survive from that date in the DRO. All 19th century registers have been microfilmed and can be consulted on fiche in all record offices in Devon. The main local studies libraries have some coverage, mainly for more recent dates, covering the area where the library is located. Poll books, which indicate the way individuals voted and were intended to prevent corrupt practices appeared between about 1695 and 1872 when the secret ballot was intoduced. They occasionally reached printed form, for example for the Exeter election of 1818 when the poll was printed by R. Cullum with the *Addresses, speeches, squibs, songs &c which were circulated during the recent election.* Relatively few poll books survive for Devon in libraries and record offices. Those that do are listed in *Poll books c1696-1772* by J.Gibson (3rd ed, 1994).

Further reading:
Historial Association. *Short guides to records: poll books* (1994)

### 3.349 District council records.
Urban and Rural District Councils were established in 1888 and replaced by District Councils in 1974. Their records, where they survive, are mostly deposited in the DRO.

## 3.35 NATIONAL ARCHIVES

The Public Record Office in Kew is England's national archive. The contents of the massive collection are summarised in the three volume *Guide to the contents of the Public Record Office* and the more recent *Current guide* (1996) which is available on microfiche. Many transcripts, calendars and lists of national archives are published by HMSO or the Public Record Office. The earliest official record publications are those by the Record Commission in the late 18th and early 19th centuries. A useful listing is to be found in *HMSO sectional list 24* which lists the titles published and outlines the coverage of many categories of records. *HMSO Sectional list 17* covers the publications of the Royal Commission on Historical Manuscripts which include many official records in private collections. Good runs of the publications covered by both these sectional lists are held in Exeter Reference and Exeter University Libraries. Publications are also available in Plymouth Reference Library.

Further reading:
Morton, A. *British national records and the local historian.* (1980).

### 3.351 Medieval records and record publications
Some of the main early series of records, many of which have been edited, calendared or listed are noted below. In parentheses are the PRO class letters and numbers, the periods for which calendars are available, and sometimes the dates for which Devon references are incorporated in the Burnet Morris Index in WSL. Other national records are held in the House of Lords Record Office. A useful source for these is *Guide to the records of Parliament* by M.F. Bond.

CHANCERY RECORDS
The Court of Chancery was the King's main centre of administration in the middle ages and a number of the main series of records have been published.

Patent rolls (C.66, calendared 1216-1578, Burnet Morris 1216-1509, 1547-57). So called because they were issued open with the great seal pendent, these include grants and leases of land, appointments to offices, licences and pardons. In 1365 for example they record the pardon granted to one Simon Bade of Barnstaple for outlawry (Cal. Pat. Rolls 1364-70, p.80).

Close rolls (C. 54 1227-1509, 1227-1447). These include writs to individuals which were folded or closed up. Contents can include the observance of treaties, repair of buildings, or payment of salaries. In 1343 for example they record the issue of orders to the bailiffs of Dartmouth and other Devon ports to arrest certain named ships (Cal. Close. Rolls 1343-6, p.129-31).

Charter rolls (C.53 1226-1515, 1226-1515). The royal charter was the writ by which the monarch made grants of lands, liberties and privileges to corporations and individuals. Thus the grant of a market and fair to Newton Poppleford in 1253 is recorded in the charter roll for 37 & 38 Henry III (Cal. rot. chart (1803), p.82)

Fine rolls (C. 60 1227-1509, 1272-1383). These include payment for writs, licences to marry, pardons and appointments of sheriffs.

Inquisitions post mortem (C.132-142 1235-1368, 1485-1649). These enquiries took place on the death of a tenant in chief under the King to establish the lands that were held. The Devon and Cornwall Record Society has published *Inquisitions post mortem: a calendar for Cornwall and Devon 1216-1649*, edited by E.A. Fry (1906) and WSL has a typescript summary of several thousand IPMs.

Early Chancery proceedings. These are covered by the PRO lists and indexes series. A special category of cases published by the Devon and Cornwall Record Society is *A calendar of early Chancery proceedings relating to Westcountry shipping 1388-1493*, edited by Dorothy M.Gardiner (1976).

EXCHEQUER RECORDS

Domesday Book (E. 31 1086). This unique survey of William the Conqueror's possessions is the oldest of the public records and has been published in facsimile or as an edited text on a number of occasions. Devon is fortunate in having in Exeter Cathedral Library a manuscript containing a fuller version covering the western counties. The Devonshire Association published the *Devonshire Domesday and geld inquest* in two volumes in 1884. This gives parallel texts of the Exchequer and Exon versions with translations. A more recent edition was published by Phillimore in 1985. Facsimiles of the Exchequer text were published by Ordnance Survey as long ago as 1862, while the

*Rex habet burgum Lideforde* ... [facsimile of Domesday entry in medieval Latin script]

### Lideforde.

Rex habet burgum Lideforde. Rex Eduuardus tenuit in dominio. Ibi sunt xxviii burgenses intra burgum et xli extra. Inter omnes reddunt regi lx solidos ad pensum, et habent ii carucatas terræ extra burgum. Ibi sunt xl. domus uastæ postquam rex uenit in Angliam. Quod si expeditio uadit uel per terram uel per mare tantum seruitii reddit quantum Barnestaple uel Totenais.—*Exch. D.* 100 (2); 1 *b.*

The king has a borough Lideforde. King Edward held it in demesne. There are twenty-eight burgesses within the borough, and forty-one without. Among them all they render to the king sixty shillings by weight, and they have two carucates of land without the borough. There are forty houses lying waste there since the king came into England. If an expedition goes by land or by sea it [*the borough*] renders as much service as Barnstaple or Totnes.

*Compiled in 1086, the Domesday Book was the first detailed survey of England. At the top is shown the facsimile from the Exchequer version for the Borough of Lydford with the 1884 Devonshire Association translation below.*

Alecto facsimile of *The Devonshire Domesday* (1988) is in colour with accompanying translations, identifications and a volume of Domesday Book studies.

Book of fees. This is also known as the Testa de Nevill and is made up of returns and lists, mainly for the period 1234-42, copied in about 1307. It is useful on the holdings of feudal tenants.

Feudal aids. This is made up of returns and surveys of holders of land between 1284 and 1431.

These and other sources were extensively used by Oswald Reichel a series of articles which appeared in the *Transactions of the Devonshire Association* between 1903 and 1922. Those unpublished at his death were issued by the Devonshire Association in ten parts with the title 'The hundreds of Devon' between 1928 and 1938. There is also a very full name index.

Pipe rolls (E.372 1130-1242). These are audits of accounts taken before the barons of the Exchequer, usually sent in by the sheriff and are arranged by county. The Pipe Roll Society has edited many records in this class which contains much local material. Thus in Michaelmas 1221 the Bishop of Exeter is shown as owing 35 marks in knights' fees, while the Abbot of Tavistock owed three marks (Pipe Roll Soc. new series, vol. 48, p.68). The transcripts are highly abbreviated.

Liberate rolls (E. 403). These contain writs by which officers of the Exchequer were ordered to make payments on behalf of the Crown.

JUDICIAL RECORDS
These include Curia Regis rolls (1189-1220), Court of Common pleas and King's Bench records.

Assize records. Dealt with the most serious crimes, such as murder and treason. Assizes in Devon were held twice yearly. The assize records for the Western Circuit survive for the period 1611-1936 in the PRO. Some local records have been calendared by J.S. Cockburn in *Western circuit assize orders 1629-1648* (1976), and for an earlier period the *Assize roll, county of Devon 1359* by A.J. Howard (1970). Little survives locally but gaol calendars for the period 1854-1919 are held in the DRO.

Chronicles and memorials. Also known as the Rolls Series; these are not archives but editions of medieval chronicles and similar historical records published during the nineteenth century. There are many references to Devon in these early sources, sets of which are held in WSL and Exeter University Library.

### 3.352 Early modern series
The record group known as State Papers is made up from the documents which accumulated in the offices of the principal secretaries of state from Tudor times onwards. Published calendars of these have been issued in various series:

Letters and papers of Henry VIII (1509-47). These cover both domestic and foreign matters and have been indexed by Burnet Morris.

State papers domestic. There is a microfilm covering the period 1547-1640 in the University of Exeter Library. They are covered by the Burnet Morris Index for the period 1547 to 1704 and there is a considerable amount of local information. Two examples must suffice: Calendar of state papers domestic 1581-90, p.665 includes an order by the Queen to the Mayor of Exeter to deliver up Philip Hart, a condemned criminal, to serve in the wars in Ireland, and the volume for 1687-9 contains on page 360 a note dated 23 November 1688 that an account of Willam of Orange's departure from Exeter had been received in London.

State papers colonial and foreign. Have also been searched by Burnet Morris as there is a considerable amount of relevant information. The same applies to the Venetian, Spanish, Scotland and Ireland series.

Committee for compounding with delinquents. Delinquents were individuals who took the royalist side during the Civil War. Burnet Morris has covered them for the whole period 1643 to 1660.

Other series of early modern records tackled by Burnet Morris include the Acts of the Privy Council (1542-1641, 1542-1627)

### 3.353 Departmental records
Treasury books and papers. The Calendars have been searched for Devon items by Burnet Morris from 1556 to 1745.

Home Office papers. The Calendars have been searched by Burnet Morris from 1760 to 1775. The Home Office records also include the census for 1841 and 1851. See section 3.353 for details.

Board of trade. This department began as the Commission for Trade and Plantations. The Journals have been looked at by Burnet Morris for the period 1708-22 and 1728-82. An important later category of records are crew lists (BT/99), some of which were transferred to the DRO in 1970-71, see DRO *Handlist no. 3* which gives details of 5000 annual returns covering the period 1863-1914.

Inland revenue. Records include registers of apprentices on which premiums were paid. Details for Crediton have been extracted in Venn's manuscript history. From 1796 to 1857 transcripts of wills were made for tax purposes (see 3.365 below). Land tax records also belong to the Inland Revenue records (see 4.33).

Tithe Commissioners. The most important group of records are the tithe apportionment surveys. See section 3.224.

Customs. Shipping registers, normally starting in 1824 with some earlier items, have been transferred from local customs houses to the DRO. Customs rolls for Exeter start in the reign of Edward II, about the same date as the records in the City archives.

### 3.353 Registrar General

This department is discussed separately as it includes two important series, the census records (from 1861, earlier records are with the Home Office papers) and civil registration (from 1837). Census enumerators' returns and the indexes to births, marriages and deaths from 1837 can be consulted for the whole country in the Family Records Centre, Myddleton Street, London EC1 (tel: 0181-392 5300).

CENSUS ENUMERATORS' RETURNS

Census enumerators' returns are the only publicly available source to provide details of every individual in a community including women and children. A census of population has been held every ten years since 1801, except for the war year of 1941. In addition a ten per cent sample census was held in 1966. The results have been published as statistical tables by the Stationery Office and are available in most large reference libraries (see section 3.173). From 1801 to 1831 the censuses were locally administered by parish overseers or clergy and any records of local population enumeration survive rarely and are scattered in local record offices. After the establishment of the General Register Office local registrars appointed enumerators to deliver forms to each household in the enumeration district allocated to them and to collect them after census night. These forms were then tabulated by the enumerator in books which formed the enumerators' returns. These provided the raw material for the totalling and statistical analysis which eventually resulted in the published census volumes. The enumerators books, which contained detailed information on individuals, were restricted for one hundred years before being released for general public consultation and microfilm copies have been produced by the Public Record Office for general sale. Those for 1841, 1851, 1861, 1871, 1881 and 1891 have so far been released and have been purchased by libraries in Devon.

Contents

The forms used to transcribe the information vary from one census to another. The 1841 census returns contain less information than the later ones, and, as they were written on blue paper, the microfilms are usually difficult to decipher.

Schedule (original form) number. From 1851.
Place (street name, house name or number).
Houses. 1841, 1861 onwards distinguish uninhabited houses.
Names. Surname and forename of those resident on census night.
Relation to head of family (wife, son, lodger etc). From 1851.
Marital condition (married, unmarried, widowed). From 1851.
Age and sex. Ages over 15 rounded down to nearest five years in 1841.
Occupation (rank,profession, employment).
Where born. County or country if outside England and Wales 1841, parish and county from 1851.
Whether blind, deaf or dumb. From 1851.
Whether imbecile or idiot. From 1871.
Employment status. From 1891.
Number of rooms. From 1891.

Institutions such as prisons, workhouses, boarding schools, hospitals and also ships have special forms.

**3** ————————————————————————————

Arrangement
In 1841 the books are arranged by hundred and then by parish within each hundred. From 1851 the arrangement is by registration district, subdivided by subdistrict, town or parish, and enumeration district. Within each enumeration district the arrangement reflects the frequently circuitous route the enumerator travelled, winding along one side of a street, into alleys, crossing the road, diverting to take in individual properties.

Indexes
No indexes were compiled at the time the census was taken. The Public Record Office has produced listings, which usually follow the arrangement of the parishes in the printed statistical tables, grouped into enumeration districts and not alphabetically by place within county. Local studies collections in Devon have produced alphabetical indexes to the parishes in their collections. The Public Record Office has provided street indexes to some of the larger towns. Some libraries have also produced street indexes to their local towns. Surname indexes in Devon have been produced in a series of booklets covering individual enumeration districts for 1851 and published by the Devon Family History Society. These are available in the main local studies collections and from the Society. There are a range of computer generated indexes to the 1881 census produced by the Mormons who have also recently completed the 1851 census for Devon..

Referencing
The system of reference adopted by the Public Record Office is as follows:

1. The **class** (to 1851 Home Office records, from 1861 Registrar General's records). 1841: HO 107, 1851: HO 107 (continues1841 numbering), 1861: RG 9, 1871: RG 10, 1881: RG 11, 1891: RG 12

2. The **piece** (book, box or bundle of documents)
This is a running number quoted after the class and an oblique stroke: e.g. RG 12/1777 (the 1891 returns for parishes in the Ilfracombe subdistrict).
In 1841 the piece is a box containing books with separate foliation: e.g. HO 107/262/9 covers Chagford for 1841.

The returns made by the Census Enumerators, gathering information for the statistical tables published in the census reports, are released after 100 years. They are the only public record which aims to list every inhabitant of the country and so are invaluable sources for local historians. This page is taken from the 1891 census (PRO RG12/1676/102) and shows the marks made when analysing the data. Crown Copyright material in the Public Record Office is reproduced by permission of the Controller of the Stationery Office.

## 3. The **folio**

In 1841 the folio number was printed on the top right of each page. Each book has a separate sequence of numbers:  e.g. HO 107/203/13 fo. 1-13 lists the inmates of Barnstaple gaol in 1841

From 1851 the folio number was stamped on the top right of each folio. Numbering runs in one sequence through all the books in each piece: e.g. RG 9/1423/99 is the first folio of the 1861 Charleton returns.

## 4. The **page**

From 1851 each book has its own pagination printed and this can be used in addition to the reference to the front (recto) or back (verso) of the folio to provide a more precise reference:  e.g RG 9/1519 fo.10 p.20.

Local libraries in Devon have usually provided their own system of reference to the reels or fiches in their individual collections.  Typically this provides a sequential number for each reel or fiche.  Finding aids usually list places alphabetically, with reference to the reel or fiche number, frequently also giving the Public Record Office number.

Holdings

WSL
1841-1891 All Devon and some border parishes in adjoining counties.

PLYMOUTH LOCAL STUDIES LIBRARY
1841-1891 Plymouth registration district.
1891 Tavistock and Okehampton registration districts.

TORQUAY LOCAL STUDIES LIBRARY
1841-1891 Torbay district.
1891 Newton Abbot, Totnes, Kingsbridge registration districts.

NORTH DEVON LOCAL STUDIES CENTRE (BARNSTAPLE)
1841-1891 Barnstaple, Bideford, South Molton, Torrington and Holsworthy registration districts.

EXMOUTH REFERENCE LIBRARY
1891 Axminster, Honiton and St. Thomas (part) registration districts

As census enumerators' returns are held in microform it is wisest to contact local studies collections in advance to reserve a microform viewer. Library staff cannot search microfilms on behalf of enquirers.

Use for education and research
As these are the fullest available listings of inhabitants of each community in the past, there is a wide range of uses to which the records can be put. For the genealogist they provide evidence of family relationships, ages and place of birth which can give clues for the appropriate parish registers or civil registration records to search for baptisms or births. For the demographic historian they give evidence of age structure, family size and migration. For the house historian they give detailed evidence of occupancy. For the social and economic historian they give evidence of occupation and education. Schools have put the returns for their community on databases to facilitate analysis by occupation, place of birth or family names. They can answer such questions as: How many children worked for a living? How many households had servants? Use of the returns can be combined with fieldwork to identify buildings listed. Beside history, the returns can cover geography, maths and information technology in the national curriculum.

Further reading:
Boreham, J.M. *The census and how to use it* (1982)
Chapman, C.R. *Pre-1841 census and population listings in the British Isles* (2nd ed, 1991)
Gibson, J.S.W. *Census returns on microfilm: a directory to local holdings* (5th ed, 1990)
Gibson, J.S.W. *Census indexes and indexing* (2nd ed, 1983)
Higgs, E. *Making sense of the census: the manuscript returns for England and Wales, 1801-1901* (1989)
Lumas, S. *Making use of the census* (1992). PRO readers guide; 1.
McLaughlin, E. *The censuses 1841-1881* (1986)
Mozley, H. *People count: teacher notes on using the Victorian census* (1991)
Nissel, M. *People count: a history of the General Register Office* (1987)
Office of Population, Censuses and Surveys. *Guide to census reports: Great Britain 1801-1966* (1977)

CIVIL REGISTRATION OF BIRTHS, MARRIAGES AND DEATHS
This was introduced in 1837 and improved on the patchy coverage of parochial and non-parochial registration of baptisms, marriages and burials. Registers are available for England and Wales back to 1837 at

the Family Records Centre, Myddleton Street London, with local registrations held at district offices throughout the country. Microfilms of the indexes to births, marriages and deaths covering the whole country from 1837 are available in the North Devon Athenaeum at Barnstaple and the Plymouth Chapel of the Mormon Church by appointment.

**3.36 ECCLESIASTICAL RECORDS**
In the past the Church played a much wider part in the regulation of society than it does today and it had considerable jurisdiction over the moral behaviour of individuals as well as requiring a considerable administrative structure to maintain its properties and estates. Most surviving ecclesiastical records for Devon are deposited in the DRO.

**3.361 Diocesan records**
These were received from the Diocese in 1954 and have a complex series of listings which are explained in a DRO leaflet. Some of the main groups include:

Bishops registers 1257-. These form the record of the official acts of the Bishops together with correspondence and other records. Those of most of the pre-Reformation bishops have been calendared, those from Bishop Walter Bronescombe in 1257 until Bishop Edmund Lacey 1455, edited by F.C. Hingeston-Randolph between 1889 and 1909, and that of Bishop Lacey, more fully edited by G.R. Dunstan and published by the Devon and Cornwall Record Society in five volumes 1963 - 1972.

Act Books of the Diocese are registers of business including alterations to churches and a range of other licences. They are in nine volumes and cover the period 1568-1734.

As can be expected, a wide range of records relate to the clergy. These include licences to preach, registers and papers relating to ordination starting in 1571, licences and registers for non-residence starting in 1804 and also records of complaints against the clergy.

Bishop's transcripts of parish registers. These are discussed under the section for parish registers (3.311). A related type of record are marriage bonds (1660-1823), allegations (1755-1842) and licences (registers 1734-1918). Licences exempted those intending to marry from the calling of banns in the parish church and were normally used if partners were not resident in the same parish or if either partner was a minor. From 1523 to 1734 licences did not have their own registers but were recorded in the Principal Registry Act Books. Typescript indexes to this scattered mass of material are available to members of the Devon and Cornwall Record Society in the Society's library in the WSL, and the DRO produce a leaflet guide to this class of records.

Church property has various types of records, including licences to alter church structures and fittings and enquries about parsonage houses. Church land or glebe is the subject of records such as glebe terriers or glebe exchanges. Records of episcopal estates have been transferred from the Church Commissioners and there is also a collection of deeds and documents relating to Exeter Cathedral as well as manor court books, leases and rentals for Bishop's manors in the diocese. See the Historical Association *Short guides to records: glebe terriers* (1994).

Bishops' visitations, records for which survive between 1622 and 1919, are regular inspections of the diocese made by the Bishop. Replies to bishops' queries prior to visitations were made by local incumbents on a range of parish matters such as dissenters, schools, the poor, population. Those for the visitation of 1821 are transcribed in *The diocese of Exeter in 1821*, edited by M. Cook (DCRS, 1960). See the Historical Association *Short guides to records: episcopal visitation books* (1994).

Beside the control over the established church, an eye was kept on non-conformist congregations with registers of licences to meeting houses (1739-1852) as well as certificates (1791-1852). The Diocese also had jurisdiction over other areas of life and among less expected classes of records are licences for schoolmasters, and surgeons.

The Bishop of Exeter's Consistory Court, 1513-1933. This dealt with ecclesiastical matters, wills, tithes and morals. The Act Books survive from 1513 and other categories of records reflect the legal nature of this body's work: depositions, exhibit books, cause papers and precedent books. The DRO has published *The records of the Bishop of Exeter's Consistory Court to 1660*, by Donald Vage (Handlist no. 1, 1981).

### 3.362 Archdeaconry records
Most of the records of the Archdeaconries of Exeter and Totnes were destroyed in 1942. The records of the Archdeaconry of Barnstaple for

the period 1570-1857 are held in NDRO. The earliest records have been edited by Peter Christie in *Of chirch-reeves, and of testamentes: the church, sex and slander in Elizabethan north Devon, 1570-1579* (1994).

Further reading:
Tarver, A. *Church court records: an introduction for family and local historians* (1995).

### 3.363 Rural deaneries
These are smaller administrative units of the diocese. Presentments, mandates and papers from rural deans survive from 1662 to the present century and records of individual deaneries, such as Ottery, are also available.

### 3.364 Nonconformist records
Registers of nonconformist congregations prior to 1837 were called in by the Registrar General and are now in the Public Record Office. DCRS has microfilms of these registers and most are included on the IGI. An excellent introduction to nonconformist registers is provided by Hugh Peskett in his *Guide to the parish and non-parochial registers of Devon and Cornwall 1538-1837* (1979). Many records are deposited in DRO and for the Methodist denominations there is a special guide by Roger F.S. Thorne, *Methodism in Devon: a handlist of chapels and their records* (DRO Handlist no. 2, 2nd ed., 1989).

### 3.365 Probate records.
These are discussed here because until 1858 most wills were proved in a variety of ecclesiastical courts depending largely on the area in which property was held. The five main courts in Devon were the three Archdeaconry courts of Totnes, Barnstaple and Exeter, the Episcopal Consistory Court of Exeter and the Episcopal Principal Registry of Exeter. All of these records were destroyed in 1942 air raids. No list survives of the wills proved in the Archdeaconry Court of Totnes; for Barnstaple there is a typescript listing in WSL, while for the other three courts there is a published calendar by E.A. Fry (British Record Society Index Library, vols 35 and 46, 1908-14), but these give no details other than name, place and year. Selections of Devon wills were summarised by Olive Moger and Sir Oswyn Murrary before the Second World War and the typescript volumes are available in WSL. Many of these wills are copies of wills proved by Devonians from the registers of the main

In the Chamber over the Hall

| | |
|---|---|
| Item one Tablebord | iii s iiii d |
| it 1 wecker Chare | xii d |
| it 1 Trunke | iii s iiii d |
| it 1 great Trunk Chest | vi s viii d |
| it 1 bedd ii bolsters 4 pillowes | iii li ii s iii d |
| it 1 Old Doust bed 1 pr of blancketts | viii s |
| it 1 bed ii bolsters 1 pyllow | |
| of Flox | xiii s iiii d |
| it 1 old Arris Coidlitt 1 Arris | |
| Carpett | iiii s vi d |
| it 2 other old Coidlitts | iii s |
| it 2 Ruggs | viii s |
| it 2 pr of Curtaines 1 old | xviii s |
| *Sum* | vi li xi s v d |

*Unfortunately most Devon probate records were destroyed during the Second World War. Apart from the wills, probate inventories provide a wealth of detail on individuals' possessions. This inventory, revealing the contents of a bedroom, is for the Exeter bookseller Michael Harte, and dates from 1615.*

English probate court, the Prerogative Court of Canterbury, whose records survive in the PRO with a series of published indexes up to the 18th century. From 1796 to 1812 copies of Devon wills are available at the PRO. DCRS has a microfilm of the PRO calendar of these wills. From 1812 to 1857 there is a complete series of copies of Inland Revenue will transcripts in the DRO. DRO also has a card index of copies of individual wills. From 1858 wills have been registered centrally at the Principal Probate registry in London, with listings available in district registries. Invaluable social documents attached to wills are probate inventories, full listings of household goods. Of the very few that survive for Devon many have been transcribed by Margaret Cash in Devon inventories of the 16th and 17th centuries (DCRS new series, vol. 11, 1966). An unusual exception to the general dearth of probate records in Devon is the parish of Uffculme, which was a peculiar of the Diocese of Salisbury. The wills and inventories in the Wiltshire Record Office have been edited by Robin Stanes and a local history group and have been published by the DCRS (1997).

Further reading:
Camp, A.J. *Wills and their whereabouts* (1963)
Gibson, J.S.W. *Probate jurisdictions: where to look for wills.* 4th ed (1994)
Historical Association. *Short guides to records: wills [and] probate inventories* (1994).

### 3.37 ESTATE AND FAMILY RECORDS

The study of manorial records is a specialist field. The court leet and view of frankpledge elected the constable and hayward, dealt with the enforcement of laws and customs. The court baron dealt with changes of copyhold, property damage and the open field system. The general administration was in the hands of a steward. By the late 17th century vestries had taken over much business formerly dealt with by the manor. Types of records include accounts (or compoti), court rolls and custumals or extents. The records of many manors are to be found in local record offices, often as part of larger estate collections or as part of the records of bodies such as the Diocese of Exeter. Records have become scattered over the centuries and a national register is maintained by the Manorial Documents Register, part of the Royal Commission on Historical Manuscripts, Quality House, Quality Court, Chancery Lane London WC2A 1HP. The register can now be consulted on the Internet (http://www.hmc.gov.uk).

Later estate records normally include surveys, rentals, maps, household accounts and legal documents relating to estates, such as inventories, marriage settlements, wills and other probate records. Title deeds and leases form a large part of estate records. Among the larger estates in DRO are Bedford (1258M), Fortescue (1262M), Rolle (96M), Peter (123M), Courtenay (1508M), Drake (346M), Kennaway (961M) and the Diocese of Exeter. NDRO holds the estates of Chichester (50/11. 1308, 1478), Pine-Coffin (63/4) and the Bideford Bridge Trust (4274, B68, BBT). Because of the complex ownership of scattered estates, many Devon estate records are held outside the county. The National Register of Archives at the Royal Commission on Historical Manuscripts will have entries for many of these.

Estate sale catalogues are important sources of information on estates. These printed and frequently illustrated items, often with detailed maps, do not always form part of the estate records but may form part of the collections of solicitors or estate agents or may be individually acquired. Libraries have some examples of these but there are extensive collections in DRO (especially 62/9 and 547B). They are currently being indexed by the Devon Gardens Trust.

Further reading:
Alcock, N.W. *Old title deeds* (1986)
Alcock, N.W. 'An east Devon manor in the later middle ages' in *Transactions of the Devonshire Association* 102 (1970) 141-187; 105 (1973) 141-190. A study of the records of Bishop's Clyst.
Dibben, A.A. *Title deeds* (Historical Association Helps for students of history, 1968)
Finberg, H.P.R. *Tavistock Abbey: a study in the social and economic history of Devon* (2nd ed 1969).
Historical Association *Short guides to records: deeds of title* (1994).
Stuart, D. *Manorial records* (1992).

### 3.38 BUSINESS AND OTHER RECORDS
Record of individual businesses only survive rarely and those deposited in record offices must serve as examples of a much wider mass of documentation. Some records survive in estate papers, for example the Iddesleigh papers contain records of the manganese mine at Upton Pyne (51/24/129). Some mining plans are also held. DRO has a number of farm account books, and solicitors' collections sometimes have

material of relevance. Other individual collections include that of Ellis, the Exeter watchmaker and shipping records in the Holman bequest. DRO has a special listing of business records.

Insurance records contain details of many thousands of individual businesses but normally the policy number must be known to locate the relevant entry in the register. Extensive collections of insurance registers are held at Guildhall Library, London and an index on microfiche to Sun and Royal Exchange policies between 1775 and 1787 is available in the Westcountry Studies Library. DRO has the registers of the West of England Insurance Company.

Trade guilds are also an important source of information for business and economic history, but the guild system was not widely developed in Devon and few records have survived. The most significant records are for the Worshipful Company of Weavers, Fullers and Shearmen of Exeter and the DRO has produced a calendar of its documents (ref: 58/7). These were used by Joyce Youings for her work *Tuckers' Hall, Exeter: the history of a provincial city company through five centuries* (1968).

### 3.4 THE LANDSCAPE

Together with the documentary record the landscape is our other major source for the past around us and there are various guides to teach us how to read it, not least the work of W.G. Hoskins. Since Professor Hoskins began his researches into Devon, archaeologists have shown that the county's landscape is made of of many elements dating back to Roman and often prehistoric times, although medieval evidence is easier to identify. This section mentions some of the sources of greatest use in interpreting the landscape.

Settlement patterns: the present-day layout of a settlement can frequently yield clues to its past history. The wide main street of towns such as Honiton may reveal the presence of a market in past centuries, the street being wide enough to accommodate stalls or even more permanent buildings, such as a butchers shambles. Lydford preserves the evidence of Saxon town planning, with grassy paths between houses along the main street representing planned side streets which were never developed in an important town which once had its own mint but was later abandoned. The burgage plots of South Zeal are a fossilised relic of a new town planned in the middle ages but which was not successful. Abandoned farmsteads may be recognised by the visible remains of earthworks, but others may have to be deduced from field names or the pattern of trackways. Surviving buildings also provide much evidence, indicating the wealth of the community. For example many Devon churches were rebuilt in the fifteenth century, a prosperous period for the wool trade. Housing developments attached to industrial undertakings in the 18th or 19th centuries may be difficult to pinpoint from historical sources but they provide in themselves very concrete evidence of the past. Examples are not just to be found in towns, such as the houses built for Heathcote's factory in Tiverton but also in villages where papermakers or other millowners may have built cottages for the millworkers. Access to local and national guides to architecture, public, industrial and vernacular, is important to be able to date and identify particular types of buildings. Section 4.2 gives more guidance on this.

Field patterns
The Braunton Great Field is a nationally known example of the medival open field system but vestiges of strip systems elsewhere can be detected on maps, through aerial photographs, or on the ground. Other special types of field systems are the Dartmoor reaves, identified as prehistoric land boundaries dating back to the Bronze Age. In places the embankments surrounding medieval deer parks or other estates can be seen crossing woodland or surviving as hedgebanks. The techniques of hedgerow dating, based on counting the number of species of tree or shrub making up a hedge, can be used to test whether a boundary is ancient, though detailed investigations at Roadford Reservoir by K.A. Westcott show that this evidence should be treated with caution.

Parks and gardens
These are a prominent feature of the Devon landscape. Often a lodge house or an elaborate gateway can reveal the entrance to a landscaped estate whose original layout may be overgrown. The Devon Gardens Trust are giving attention to this aspect of our heritage and an important guide is provided by Todd Gray's *The garden history of Devon* (1995).

Roads and tracks
While ley lines should be treated with the greatest of caution, normally being the result of using a ruler and compasses on a map rather than fieldwork, there are fossilised road networks that can be deduced from

the ground. Sometimes a modern road will diverge from the original route to divert around a steep obstacle, the original line being marked by a green lane. A good example of this is the main road westward from Tavistock to Gunnislake. Care should be taken to distinguish apparent trackways from mill leats, deserted railways, or even roads and runways connected with Second World War installations. Here early editions of Ordnance Survey maps and the tithe survey can be helpful.

Land charters
These and other early perambulations of boundaries often give details that can be checked out by fieldwork. The charters are largely pre-conquest grants of land, commonly by the monarch. They frequently give details of boundaries and boundary marks which are still very descriptive of natural and man-made elements in the landscape. A listing is given by H.P.R. Finberg in *The early charters of Devon and Cornwall* (2nd ed, 1963). They were worked on by W.G. Hoskins in *The westward expansion of Wessex* (1960) and more recently by Della Hooke in *Pre-conquest charter-bounds of Devon and Cornwall* (1994). For a more recent period glebe terriers sometimes include a perambulation of the parish boundaries described topographically with reference to adjoining estates. Parish boundaries, established in medieval times and marked on larger scale Ordnance Survey maps, are often revealing about the age of trackways and field boundaries on their course.

Place-names
Place-name studies can also complement fieldwork for this early period and still the most comprehensive source here is *The place-names of Devon*, published by the English Place-Name Society in 1931.

Fieldwork
The history of the landscape can only be fully unravelled by 'getting your boots muddy', as Professor Hoskins recognised long ago. Farmers often know of features on their land which no historian or archaeologist has previously recorded.

There are a number of types of records that are especially useful in conjunction with fieldwork. Maps have already been mentioned and a related source is aerial photographs. There are collections of these in most libraries, but coverage is normally limited as they are expensive to acquire. Libraries have acquired two complete fly-overs of Devon, one made in 1981 and the other in 1993. See section 3.215 for further detail on this source.

Many of the results of fieldwork are published in the journals of national and local archaeological societies, such as the Devon Archaeological Society. Reference to more than 55 000 recorded items of archaeological and historic interest, linked to an Ordnance Survey map base, is maintained by the Devon Sites and Monuments Register at County Hall, Exeter. This is open to the public during normal office hours by prior appointment only (tel: 01392-382266).

Further reading:
Hoskins, W.G. *The making of the English landscape* (Rev. ed. with commentary by C.Taylor, 1988).
    *Hedges and local history.* (1971).
    *Archaeology of the Devon landscape.* (1980).
Ordnance Survey. *Field archaeology: some notes for beginners.* (5th ed, 1973).

# PART 4
# SOME THEMES

## 4.1 PARISH AND TOWN HISTORY

The best general guide to manuscript and printed sources is *Sources for English local history* by W.B. Stephens. Fieldwork is also important and examination of the present-day community and its environment should accompany work with documents. WSL, DRO and some other collections produce leaflet guides to sources for parish history. Information indexes are held in major libraries and take a variety of forms (see section 3.118). The largest of these is the Burnet Morris Index, an an index of about one million references to Devon persons, places and subjects compiled between 1915 and 1940 held in WSL. It contains many references to periodical articles and publications of the Public Record Office. Check in the place section (drawers 292-391) under the name of the parish and also in the name section (drawers 1-291) for official publications. A leaflet guide to the use of this complex index is available. The Sites and Monuments Register at County Hall maintains a list of archaeological and historical sites (3.4) and local museums, libraries and historical societies may also have material which is not to be found in the larger centralised collections.

### 4.11. BOOKS AND PAMPHLETS

Local studies libraries normally have catalogues which list the books and pamphlets which they hold relating to a specific locality. In addition they will hold copies of the bibliographies noted in section 3.11. Where there is no published history of a parish some detail may be found in the church guide. Unpublished surveys of all churches in Devon were made by Davidson c.1840 and Cresswell c.1920. Both surveys are in WSL with microfiches and extracts in other locations. County histories (3.12) and guidebooks (3.13) will have sections on many communities throughout Devon. In particular the second volume of Lysons has a description of every parish in alphabetical order. Extracts from Lysons are included in the WSL cuttings files, so may be found in parish packs in branch libraries. General reference works with sections relating to the Westcountry are to be found in the general library collections.

## 4.12. DIRECTORIES

These survive for larger towns from 1783 onwards, often only on microfilm. From 1850 to 1939 the county directories have a separate entry for every parish in Devon giving, besides a list of residents and tradesmen, concise historical and descriptive notes. They are held in the larger local studies collections. See section 3.14 for more details.

## 4.13. NEWSPAPERS

Local studies libraries in Devon hold local newspapers in original or in microform for every year since 1737 with some coverage for the period 1715-31. Some newspapers have been indexed or cut for parish files. See section 3.15 for fuller details. Where newspapers have been microfilmed the original copies will not be produced by libraries. There are files containing newspaper cuttings and other notes for most Devon parishes in the main local studies collections. Those in WSL have been compiled since the 1920s and have been microfilmed for other local studies collections with extracts in parish packs in branch libraries.

## 4.14. PERIODICALS

Periodical articles are an important source for detailed studies of a locality. The *Transactions of the Devonshire Association* has cumulated indexes to the first 100 volumes and other periodicals also have cumulated indexes or indexes to individual volumes. A computer database of periodical articles can be consulted in the larger local studies libraries. See sections 3.16, 3.112.

## 4.15 OFFICIAL PUBLICATIONS

Government reports and returns often include sections relating to individual localities. Full indexes of sessional papers are available in the Exeter Reference Library and Exeter University Library. Larger libraries have collections of local acts of Parliament. A selection of House of Commons and Command Papers is held in the larger local studies collections, including census tables, Charity Commissioners Reports, and the 1873 return of owners of land. See section 3.17 for fuller details. Local government publications are especially useful for the period since the Second World War. A good range is held in the main local studies collections, but they are a complex form of publication and it is difficult to locate information on specific communities unless special planning studies have been produced, for example *Colyton conservation area* jointly produced by Devon County Council and East Devon District Council in 1977. Local government publications are normally listed under the issuing body (county, district or town council). Libraries hold sets of council minutes, sometimes only since the reorganization of 1974. Fuller sets of earlier council minutes are available in DRO. See section 3.174.

### 4.16 ARCHIVES

National archive publications, particularly the calendars of patent rolls and state papers domestic, contain many local references, as do the reports of the Historical Manuscripts Commission (see section 3.35). The Burnet Morris Index covers many but not all of the PRO and HMC publications, collections of which can be found in the Exeter Reference Library and Exeter University Library. The DRO has extensive collections of local archives for the county. Many categories of records can contain information on a parish apart from the parish collections themselves, which are detailed in section 3.31.

### 4.17. INHABITANT LISTS

These form the raw material for a wide range of demographic and social studies. Local studies libraries have the census enumerators' on microfilm for 1841-1881 and on microfiche for 1891 (see section 3.354). Other inhabitant lists include transcripts of parish registers, 1538-1837 (see section 3.311), the protestation returns of 1641, muster rolls, especially 1569, and tax and rate assessments. There are fuller details in section 4.3 on sources for family history.

### 4.18. MAPS (see section 3.22)

These are invaluable for showing the layout of the community in earlier times but it is not normally possible to obtain detailed maps earlier than 1765. Besides street plans of the larger towns and early engraved county maps there is good coverage of Devon at a scale of 1:63 360 (one inch to one mile) or larger as follows:

| 1765 | 1 in to 1 mile | Donn's survey |
|------|----------------|---------------|
| 1784-1809 | 2 , 3 or 6 in to 1 mile | Ordnance Survey drafts |
| 1809-1972 | 1 in to 1 mile | Ordnance Survey |
| 1826 | 1 in to 1 mile | Greenwood's survey |
| 1864-1890 | 6 in to 1 mile and 1:2500 | OS 1st edition |
| 1855-1892 | 1:500 etc | OS town plans |
| 1888-1962 | 1 in to 40 ft | Goad insurance (Exeter & Plymouth only) |
| 1905-1939 | 6 in to 1 mile and 1:2500 | OS 2nd ed. & revisions |
| 1945-date | 1:2500 and 1:1250 | OS national grid |
| 1945-date | 6 in to 1 mile or 1:10 000 | OS national grid |
| 1945-date | 1:25 000 | OS Pathfinder series |
| 1974-date | 1:50 000 | OS Landranger series |

Tithe maps and apportionments, mostly dating from about 1840 and other plans are deposited in the DRO.

**4.19. ILLUSTRATIONS**
Few local illustrations are found for the period before about 1775. Illustrations can be difficult to locate so prior enquiry is advisable. See section 3.21 for fuller details.

## 4.2. HISTORY OF BUILDINGS

Sources for house history can be found in the larger local studies libraries and record offices.

It is rare to be able to piece together a detailed history of smaller properties. A start should be made with the deeds and an examination of the architectural style. Take care to distinguish the name of the property from the existing fabric of the house. A house may have been rebuilt several times since the name of the property or estate was first recorded in medieval sources. It is also advisable to check the deeds of the property at the outset, if a detailed investigation is to be undertaken. Even if these do not go back very far in time, they may provide evidence of the break-up of a larger estate or point to earlier deeds or manorial or estate records which may survive in record offices. The division into types of houses which follows is used as a convenient way of introducing the various sources and the sections overlap to a considerable extent.

**4.21. LARGER NAMED PROPERTIES**

The following sources should be checked:

(a) LIBRARY CATALOGUES for published books and pamphlets (see 3.118).

(b) BIBLIOGRAPHIES (see 3.11), especially the *Devon Union List*.

(c) SURVEYS OF HISTORIC BUILDINGS. The Devon volume of Nikolaus Pevsner's *Buildings of England* series, extensively revised and extended by Bridget Cherry (1989) is available in all main local collections. A compendium of Pevsner's *Buildings of England* compiled by Michael Good on CD-ROM (1995) allows searches to be made by type of architectural feature, place, period or artist. A copy is held in Exeter Reference Library. The Department of National Heritage's *Lists of Buildings of Special Architectural or Historic Interest* are available for all Devon in WSL and district council planning offices hold *Lists* for relevant parishes. The Royal Commission on Historical Monuments has not yet covered Devon. Todd Gray's book *The garden history of Devon: an illustrated guide to sources* (1995) gives details of sources in libraries and record offices for over 200 houses and estates in Devon.

(d) PLACE-NAME DICTIONARIES. The most comprehensive of these is *The place-names of Devon* published by the English Place-Name Society in 1931. They give early forms of the names of properties and their etymology. Many of the Public Record Office documents referred to in these dictionaries have been published (see section 3.35) and are available in large general reference collections. Domesday Book is often referred to in this connection and some editions have sections identifying place-names.

(e) PERIODICAL INDEXES. These may refer to articles of relevance. The *Transactions of the Devonshire Association* have cumulated indexes to the first 100 volumes. *Country Life* publishes occasional cumulated indexes to town and country houses and gardens. See section 3.112 for details of other periodical indexes. The Burnet Morris Index in WSL is useful for details of properties. Check in the place section under the name of the parish. Illustrations in *The Builder* are covered in the *Builder illustrations index* 1843-1883 compiled by Robert Thorne and Ruth Richardson (1994). There is a county index. A file of *The Builder* is available in Exeter Reference Library but it is best checked once the date of building, alteration or restoration is fairly closely known.

(f) LOCAL OR COUNTY HISTORIES AND GUIDE BOOKS. These may mention the property. Check in the place section of the Library catalogues and bibliographies to see what is available. See sections 3.12 and 3.13 for more details.

(g) PARISH CUTTINGS FILES. Most Devon parishes are covered by such a file in WSL and many branch libraries. See section 3.151.

(h) ILLUSTRATIONS. Prints are listed in *Devon topographical prints, 1660-1870* by J.V. Somers Cocks. The major local studies collections hold topographical prints, photographs, postcards and some original drawings. About 200 larger houses are illustrated in *Devonshire: historical, descriptive, biographical* by F.J. Snell (1907). There is an index to illustrations on p.207. The microfiches of the Francis Frith collection of Devon photographs, containing 15 000 scenes are available in Devon, and a place listing is available. Books of historic illustrations can also be useful. Illustrations of over 2000 English country houses in 107 volumes of country views published between 1715 and 1872, and in other sources, are indexed in the *Country house index* compiled by John Harris (2nd ed 1979). See section 3.21 for more details on illustrations.

(i) SALE PARTICULARS. Some sale catalogues of estates are held by most of the larger local studies libraries but there are also considerable collections in DRO. The Devon Gardens Trust is engaged in indexing this class of material in record offices for information on garden history. See section 3.37.

### 4.22. SMALLER PROPERTIES
(a) TRADE DIRECTORIES. These are particularly useful for urban houses when street numbers are given or there is a street arrangement, which can be found for larger towns from the 1870s. A union listing of trade directories in the main Devon libraries is available. See section 3.14.

(b) MAPS AND PLANS. These can be useful for establishing approximate dates of construction or variations in the ground plan. There is coverage of Devon at a scale of one-inch-to-a-mile or larger from 1765. For details see 3.22 and 4.1.

(c) TITHE MAPS AND APPORTIONMENTS. These are held in DRO. Produced around 1840 they include a large scale plan for each parish with plots numbered referring to a schedule with details of owner, occupier, area and valuation. See section 3.224. The Record Office may also have other manuscript plans of the parish.

(d) CENSUS ENUMERATORS' RETURNS. Microfilms are available for 1841, 1851, 1861, 1871, 1881 and 1891 in the main local studies collections. Staff have compiled parish indexes and there are street indexes for some larger towns. Using information from other sources, such as the tithe apportionment or electoral registers, you may be able to locate the property and identify the occupiers. See section 3.354.

(e) ELECTORAL REGISTERS. The main run of these from 1832 is in DRO. Libraries also have partial runs. The arrangement is sometimes by name and sometimes by street. See section 3.348.

(f) RATE AND TAX RECORDS. The Land Tax for 1780-1832 is in DRO, with other tax and rating records. Transcribed and published records are available for many such lists - see section 4.33. A collection of rating and other records transcribed by C.A. Fursdon is held in the WSL, with microfiches in other local studies collections. Unlike the Land Tax, many such records only list names of persons and not the property.

(g) NEWSPAPERS. Advertisements can give details of properties for sale or to let. In WSL the *Exeter Flying Post* has been indexed from 1763 to 1885. Relevant entries can be found under the headings Houses, Farms, Manors and Fields. There is also an index to property names for 1763-1835. See 3.15 for details of other newspaper indexes.

(h) OTHER RECORDS. These vary depending on the type of property. Charity Commissioners' reports contain information on almshouses. Insurance records cover industrial and private properties and insurance policies may give a valuation of the property, see section 3.38. Probate records may be of value, especially if inventories are attached. Most Devon probate records were destroyed in 1942. Some published transcripts and indexes are available, see section 3.36. Some inventories have been published by the Devon and Cornwall Record Society (new series, vol. 11). Tracing ownership of a property may involve genealogical research, see section 4.3.

For most houses the precise date of construction cannot be ascertained and architectural evidence will have to used. A local study is *Devon building: an introduction to local traditions*, a collection of essays edited by Peter Beacham (rev. ed., 1995).

Further reading:

Brunskill, R.W. *Illustrated handbook of vernacular architecture* (3rd ed, 1987)

Harvey, J.H. *Sources for the history of houses* (1974).

Iredale, D. *Discovering your old house* (1977).

### 4.3 FAMILY AND POPULATION HISTORY

The study of one's own family is frequently a lead into the wider study of local history. Genealogical materials are available in the main local studies collections and in the Mormon family history centres. Original sources are normally held in DRO. Libraries and record offices produce leaflet guides and also stock books of guidance but staff is not available in libraries or record offices to undertake genealogical research on behalf of enquirers. DRO runs a record searching service which will undertake research for a fee. Fuller details are available from Devon Record Office, Castle Street, Exeter EX4 3PU (tel: 01392-384253). It should be noted that, because of migration, the local record office may not be the most suitable place to conduct research for one's own ancestry.

The Devon Family History Society exists to provide a focus for individuals working in the field of genealogy. Their quarterly journal *The Devon Family Historian* gives current details of membership and officers and can be inspected in local studies libraries. The Society also runs the Tree House in Exeter and maintains a register of members' interests. Attention is also drawn to the collections of the Devon and Cornwall Record Society, consisting largely of transcripts of parish registers and other genealogical sources, deposited in WSL for the use of the Society's members. A handlist of the collections is available for purchase and membership can be taken out in WSL. See section 1.3 of *Local studies in Devon: a guide to resources* for details of genealogical collections.

Much genealogical material is only available on microform. Researchers are strongly advised to book reading equipment in advance.

## 4.31. Indexes to existing research

To avoid wasteful duplication of research check indexes to printed pedigrees and family histories. Three of the most exhaustive printed listings are: *The genealogist's guide* by George W. Marshall (1893), *A genealogical guide* by J.B. Whitmore (1953), *The genealogist's guide* by G.B. Barrow (1977). Libraries hold many studies of individual families, normally listed at the Dewey number 929.2, as well as biographies and biographical dictionaries. The Burnet Morris Index of Devon persons, places and subjects, housed in the WSL has a very full listing of family names to 1940. A leaflet guide to this complex index is available. There are also extensive family cuttings files in WSL. *Devon: a genealogical bibliography* by Stuart A. Raymond lists published sources on a wide range of topics, with a listing of family histories in the second volume.

Many of the references in these sources will be to material held in general reference collections which often have extensive collections of biographical material, including *The Dictionary of National Biography, The Complete Peerage* by G.E. Cockayne and runs of such sources as Burke's and Debrett's peerages, *Burkes Landed Gentry, The Gentleman's Magazine* and the publications of the Harleian Society and the Public Record Office, all containing much local information.

## 4.32 Sources for genealogical research

If no previous research has been traced you are advised to check the following sources, all of which indicate family relationships:

(a)  CIVIL REGISTRATION RECORDS. These are available for England and Wales back to 1837 at the Family Records Centre, Myddleton Street, London, with local registrations held at district offices throughout the country. It is important to check these records first because of their completeness and the fact that they normally suggest a place of residence in the period 1841-91 which can then be checked on the census enumerators' returns. Indexes to births, marriages and deaths covering the whole country from 1837 are available in the North Devon Athenaeum at Barnstaple and the Plymouth Chapel of the Mormon Church by appointment.

(b)  CENSUS ENUMERATORS' RETURNS. Microfilms are available in WSL and for the whole registration county of Devon for 1841, 1851, 1861, 1871, 1881 and 1891 and in larger libraries for their area of the county. An index to parishes has been compiled by staff and surname indexes for the 1851 census have been compiled by the Devon Family History Society. A name index for the whole of Devon is available on microfiche for the 1881 census, compiled by the Mormons, who have also completed a similar index for 1851, and street indexes are available for some larger towns. From 1851 the place of birth is given, indicating which church registers should be searched. For further details on censuses see section 3.354.

(c) CHURCH REGISTERS. Transcripts of parish and non-parochial registers are held in WSL and other large libraries in Devon. See section 3.311 for fuller details. The main local guide is *Guide to the Parish and Non-parochial Registers of Devon and Cornwall, 1538-1837* by H. Peskett, although the Record Office holdings are now much more comprehensive (refer to their handlist). Larger libraries have the Mormons' *International Genealogical Index* for Devon, with details of over two million baptisms and marriages indexed for several hundred parish and non-parochial registers in the region, mainly for the period 1538-1837. The *IGI* for the British Isles is held in the main reference libraries in Devon. Monumental inscriptions are also available but there is not yet any extensive coverage for Devon although the Devon Family History Society are publishing transcripts.

(d) WILLS. Most Devon wills were destroyed during the Second World War. DRO has an index to surviving copy wills and the estate duty will transcripts for the period 1811-1857. Indexes and calendars of many wills have been published. The abstracts of Devon wills made by Sir Oswyn Murray and O. Moger before the Second World War are held in WSL. See also section 3.36.

(e) INQUISITIONS POST MORTEM. These are a major source for the period before parish registers begin. About 3000 for the Westcountry from the 13th to the 17th centuries have been calendared in typescript and held in WSL. See also section 3.35.

(f) VISITATION PEDIGREES. Printed editions are held in the major libraries. They are normally entered in catalogues under the heading College of Arms. The heralds drew up pedigrees during the 16th and 17th centuries to establish the right to bear arms.

## 4.33. Major inhabitant lists

These do not normally include details of family relationships. Lists of inhabitants have been compiled for many purposes, mainly connected with the raising of money, and are of considerable value to the demographer, genealogist and social historian. Because of the varying circumstances of their compilation their comprehensiveness varies. The user should ask: Why were they compiled? Who was listed? Who was omitted? How reliable are they? A good listing of published transcripts and other items about inhabitant lists is in the section on official lists of names in *Devon: a genealogical bibliography* vol 1 by Stuart A. Raymond (1994). The list below is arranged in rough chronological order.

1086 Domesday book. A basic source but this unique survey of land tenure contains very few individual names. The most generally available modern edition is: *Domesday book, 9: Devon*, edited by C. & F. Thorn (1985). See 3.351.

1234-42 Testa de Nevill. Also known as the *Book of Fees* this is one of the earliest available tax lists, a country-wide survey of landowners. The Devon section is transcribed in: *Transactions of the Devonshire Assocation* 30 (1898), p.203-37.

1290-1334 Lay subsidies. The fullest of these for Devon is *The Devonshire lay subsidy of 1332*, edited by A.M. Erskine (1969)

1377-1381 Poll taxes. A valuable source for the student of medieval population but no 'particular accounts' for 1377, giving the the names of those assessed, appears to survive for Devon.

1520-1650 Muster rolls. Lists of persons liable to serve in the armed forces. Among the best for Devon is *The Devon muster roll for 1569*, edited by T.L.Stoate (1977)

1524-1525 Great subsidy. The most significant of the later lay subsidies, published for Devon is *Devon lay subsidy rolls, 1524-7*, edited by T.L. Stoate (1979). Later tax assessments, including the 1581 subsidy, assessments of 1642, 1647 and 1660, and the poll tax of 1660, are transcribed in *Devon taxes, 1581-1660*, edited by T.L. Stoate (1988). Those for Exeter are included with similar assessments and listings in *Tudor Exeter: tax assessments 1489-1595*, edited by Margery Rowe for the Devon and Cornwall Record Society (1977).

1538-1837 Parish registers. These were initiated by an order of Thomas Cromwell and provide registers of baptisms, marriages and burials in each parish. See 3.311 for fuller detail. Various guides to local history and demography indicate the demographic uses to which parish registers can be put. The month of baptism enables seasonality to be established although baptisms are not the same as births and were often delayed by bad weather or religious festivals. From 1754 when partners had to sign, crude literacy rates can be established. Comparing marriage dates with dates of first baptism, pre-nuptial conception rates can be arrived at. Burial registers can also be used to plot seasonality, and for evidence of epidemics.

16th-19th century Parish rates. A number of parish rates have been transcribed in typescript by C.A. Fursdon. The original set is in WSL with print-outs in the parish files available in local branch libraries and schools. Original parish rates are held in DRO. See section 3.312.

1641-1642 Protestation returns. All adult male subjects were required to swear an oath of allegiance to the crown. The result is one of the fullest inhabitant lists before the 19th century census returns. The Devon returns are transcribed as: *The Devon protestation returns, 1641*, edited by A.J. Howard (1973). A cross thus + indicates those who signed with a cross where original returns survive. This provides rare early evidence of the extent of literacy.

1641-1677 Poll tax. The Devon poll tax for 1660 and various earlier assessments for Devon are included in *Devon taxes, 1581-1660*, edited by T.L. Stoate (1988). Exeter taxes for the same period are covered in *Exeter in the seventeeth century: tax and rate assessments 1602-1699*, edited by W.G. Hoskins for the Devon and Cornwall Record Society (1957).

1662-1689 Hearth tax. *Devon hearth tax return, Lady Day 1674*, edited by T.L. Stoate (1982). These returns give little detail but provide some indication of relative wealth as the number of hearths in each household are given. See the Historical Association *Short guide to records: hearth tax returns* (1994).

1692-19th cent Land tax. This was instituted by an Act of 1693 and the assessments give the name and status of the landowner, but not his occupation, the name of the occupier, the name and brief description of the property, amount assessed. Assessments may be quarterly, half yearly or yearly. A good set for Devon survives in the DRO for the period 1780-1832. DRO publish a guide to Land Tax Records.

1696-1868 Poll books. Relatively few survive for Devon. Those that do are normally listed in the catalogues of the main local studies collections. See section 3.348.

1781-20th cent Trade directories. See section 3.14 for fuller details. A list of holdings in the major Devon libraries is available.

1832-date Electoral registers. The main set for the county is in DRO who have microfilmed those for the period 1832-1900. Local studies collections have some recent coverage. For the 19th century, suffrage was limited by property qualifications and women were of course also excluded from the registers. See section 3.348.

1841-1891 Census returns. For fuller details see section 3.354.

c1763 to date Newspapers. See section 3.16 for fuller details.

Further information on individuals can be found in a variety of sources depending on the period, field of activity or place of residence. Parish or town histories, histories of houses, and books on particular industries may all contain information. Other sections of this guide may help, as will *Devon: a genealogical bibliography* by Stuart A.Raymond.

Further reading:
Hey, D. *Family history and local history in England.* (Longman, 1987).
Pelling, G. *Beginning your family history.* 4th ed. (Countryside Books, 1987).

### 4.4 FARMING HISTORY

Agricultural surveys: The earliest of these date from the late 18th century and are a first recourse for agricultural historians. The chief ones for Devon, all of which have been reprinted, are:

Fraser, R. *General view of the county of Devon* (Macrae, 1794, repr 1970)

Vancouver, C. *General view of the agriculture of the county of Devon* (1808, repr 1969)

Marshall, W. *The rural economy of the West of England* (Nicol, 1796, repr 1970)

Marshall, W. *Review and abstract of the county reports to the Board of Agriculture* (1818, repr 1969).

These early reviews are discussed by Sarah Wilmot in 'The scientific gaze: agricultural improvers and the topography of South-West England' in *Topographical writers in south-west England* (University of Exeter, 1996) 105-135. These have a broad geographical scope although most have sections on specific regions. For more local studies there are a variety of sources:

Trade directories: from 1850 to 1939 these list farmers and other agricultural industries both in each parish and in classified sections at the back of each volume.

Census returns: between 1841 and 1891; these give details of agricultural labourers in each parish as well as indicating their place of birth. Sometimes there is also an indication of the acreage farmed.

Newspapers: these contain market reports as regular features and give details of farms and estates for sale or lease. See section 3.15 for details of which newspapers have been indexed.

Farm account books & records: these only survive rarely. See the 'Farming history' leaflet produced by the Devon Record Office in Exeter and 'Sources for farms and farming', a leaflet produced by the North Devon Record Office for examples.

Estate and manorial records: these often contain accounts, rentals and surveys, sometimes with plans. Again the Record Office leaflets provide additional detail. Printed sale catalogues often provide detailed descriptions of farms on estates.

Maps: the tithe surveys of about 1840 are the first consistently to show field boundaries and land use. They can be compared with the Ordnance Survey six inch and 1:2500 maps, which normally commence for Devon in the 1880s, to show changes in field layout. The surveyors' drafts of the Ordnance Survey in the early 19th century only show schematic field boundaries. Enclosure awards with accompanying plans occur relatively rarely in Devon with about 80 documents for the period 1804-1923 in Devon Record Office. Twentieth century surveys, such as the Land Utilisation Survey are normally only available at a scale of one inch to a mile.

Parish records: these can be very useful with such sources as poor law apprenticeships as agricultural labourers.

Consistory Court records: these are mainly useful for tithe cases.

Probate records: these survive sparsely for Devon (see section 3.365), but probate inventories often include equipment, livestock and crops. Published examples are in *Devon inventories*, Devon and Cornwall Record Society (1966).

Quarter sessions: relevant series include the return of corn prices Q/S 124 1733-1811.

Devon County Council: the County Agricultural Committee from 1907 and various other committees contain relevant material, and agriculture has been one of the key issues in county development and structure plans since 1952. Since the 1960s the University of Exeter Agricultural Economics Unit has also been producing reports on various aspects of farming in the region.

Photographs: it may be difficult to locate relevant items in collections which are frequently arranged by place rather than theme and concentrate on towns and village centres, but the Beaford Archive in Barnstaple has many rural photographs of north Devon and items may be found in other collections.

Further reading:
Edwards, C. *Farming: sources for local historians* (Batsford, 1991)
Stanes, R. *The old farm* (Devon Books, 1990)

## 4.5 TRANSPORT HISTORY

Books: there is a wealth of published material on railways, a standard history being *Regional history of the railways of Great Britain, vol. 1: the West Country* by David St. John Thomas (6th ed, 1988). There is a major railway studies library in Newton Abbot Library. Few original records survive locally as the early railways were private undertakings before nationalisation.

On road transport two recent basic titles are: Michael Hawkins *Devon roads* (1988) and Dorian Gerhold *Road transport before the railways* (1993), a study of the carrier network between London and the Westcountry. Newspapers advertise carrier services and mail coaches from the 18th century and often contain detailed accounts of the progress on railway construction and the celebrations when new lines were opened. Trade directories list carriers, coaches and give details of postal services. Maps are an obvious source.

The most detailed Ordnance Survey plans give railway track layouts, but they often show roads and railways before construction, sometimes marking lines which were never actually completed. In DRO deposited plans cover roads, railways, canals and tramways. These were intended to accompany local acts of Parliament. In the case of road improvement acts, these often extend to the level of tolls to be levied by the turnpikes. Turnpike trustees managed many roads in the later 18th and 19th centuries but not all their records survive in Devon. Details of rights of way, often the result of extensive research, are maintained by the County Council.

There is often considerable detail on bridges. The records of bridge wardens and trusts sometimes extend back several centuries. Quarter sessions were responsible for roads and bridges from 1592 and in the parish records can be found the papers of the local surveyors of highways mainly from the 18th and 19th centuries. In DRO a few records of highway boards survive for the 1860s to 1890s. An unusual modern source in DRO are motor taxation records which survive for the County and for Exeter from 1903.

Canal documents survive in private records. Exeter City Council has many records relating to Exeter Canal. There are a series of books on the main canals in Devon and a regional survey is C.A. Hadfield's *The canals of south west England* (1984).

Sources for maritime history can be summarised quite easily since the appearance of the standard *New maritime history of Devon* (1993-94). This is supported by the papers of a conference held when the history was under discussion: *Sources for a new maritime history of Devon,* edited by David Starkey (1987). There are several papers with a maritime theme in the Exeter papers in economic history series. In local newspapers can be found regular details of shipping movements and there is an index of ships in the index to the *Exeter flying post* from 1763 which is held in WSL. Records which may be used by researchers into maritime history include shipping registers, crew lists and customs records, examples of all of which can be found in DRO. The South West Maritime History Society exists to unite those interested in this field. They publish *Maritime South West* and a newsletter.

# PART 5
# TECHNIQUES

## 5.1. READING AND INTERPRETING DOCUMENTS

Working with original documents requires the surmounting of three main obstacles: handwriting, language and content. There is a wide range of different hands and a careful seventeenth century hand can be more legible than a twentieth century scrawl. The building up of sets of upper and lower case alphabets for individual hands can help in the deciphering of individual words and care should be taken to establish whether a particular word might be an abbreviation or an unusual spelling - orthography was standardised much later in written hands than in printed books. There are three selections of local documents by the DRO which include facsimiles, transcripts and, in some cases translations: *Documents of local history: a selection of papers on Devon's past* (1969), *Oakum: strands drawn from the maritime history of Devon* (1970), and *Nos voisins d'Outre-Manche* (1973). These can all give useful practice. Most modern records are in English, but Latin lingered on in some ecclesiastical records until the early 18th century. In some medieval documents French can also be found. Many early documents are largely formulaic and a detailed knowledge of the language need not necessarily stand in the way of getting the gist of the contents. It is important to know the nature of the document being examined, its administrative background and thus what is implied by the forms of words used. Such knowledge will also help with an awareness of what is included in a particular type of record, for example the scope of the hearth tax or the information required by the Tithe Commissioners. The Historical Association's *Short guides to records* series is useful here.

Further reading:
Baxter, J.H. *Medieval Latin word-list* (1947)
Buck, W.S.B. *Examples of handwriting 1550-1650* (1965)

Hector, L.C. *The handwriting of English documents* (2nd ed, 1980)
MacLaughlin, E. *Reading old handwriting* (2nd ed, 1987)
Munby, L. *Reading Tudor and Stuart handwriting* (1988)
Newton, K.C. *Medieval local records: a reading aid* (1986)
Stuart, D. *Latin for local and family historians* (1995)
Thoyts, E.C. *How to read old documents* (1980)

### 5.2. INDEXING DOCUMENTS

Indexing is not as easy as it sounds and some of the computer programs simply provide undifferentiated strings of page numbers after each heading. Many people for this reason prefer to use manual card indexing systems but, with many word processing systems providing indexing facilities, consideration should be given to using these aids, while at the same time realising that manual editing will normally be necessary.

Indexers should look out for three main features in the documents they index: personal names, place and other proper names, and subject terms. Depending on the type of document being indexed these may be sorted into the same or separate sequences and there may on occasion be other indexes where appropriate, for example a chronological index for such persons as office holders.

There are a number of factors to be considered:

The form of personal names. Normally these are inverted to bring the surname to the front, but for medieval times the forename may also be significant. Will the surnames be indexed as they stand or will the form of surname be standardised? Standardisation is helpful for the earlier period but should be used with caution from the 18th century onward. In either case 'see' or 'see also' references should be used. Would a brief identification be helpful, e.g. 'Brice, Andrew (printer, Exeter)' or 'fl. 1475'? This takes time but can make the index much more helpful and can repay dividends when prolific entries have to be split. Also, if a database is used to produce the index, it might be possible automatically to generate place indexes under Exeter and subject indexes under Printers for the said Andrew Brice.

The form of place-names. Again the question of standardisation must be raised and authorities such as Ordnance Survey can be adopted as a model. Where appropriate, reference from the form of names found in the original documents should be given. As with personal names, some form of identification may be useful, e.g. 'Portledge (house, Alwington)'.

Subject entries.

These are in many ways the most difficult and hence the most neglected type of indexing. The choice of terms is difficult, as is the level of specificity and form of subdivision. There is a danger in being too general in the choice of terms e.g. 'Trade' instead of 'Wine trade'. It is difficult for a person looking for something specific to know under what more general term the items may have been placed. Avoid inverted terms wherever possible, cross references can always be given e.g. ''Transport, road. See Road transport'. Prefer concrete to abstract terms, e.g. 'Birds' rather than 'Ornithology'.

The need to avoid strings of undifferentiated numbers means that thought should be given to a consistent way of subdividing larger headings. For example, for a person, the page numbers could be given in numerical order with a brief explanation e.g.:

Birth, 1; early years, 2-3; schooling 4-6 [etc.]

An alternative is a form of subject grouping e.g.

Characteristics: generosity, 27; wit, 45.
Travels: Cevennes, 48; Pyrenees, 74

Further reading:
Collison, R.L. *Indexes and indexing* (4th ed, 1972)
Mulvany, Nancy C. *Indexing books* (1994)
Wellisch, H. *Indexing from A-Z* (2nd ed, 1996)

### 5.3. STATISTICS

Statistics should be included in tables whever possible, although selected statistics can be cited in the body of the text. Work with sources such as census returns and parish registers can soon build up considerable bodies of statistical information. Family reconstitution is a valuable exercise based on parish registers and other sources. From this the length of residency of families within a parish can be calculated as well as average ages at marriage, average family size, infant mortality rates and a range of other demographic data. Useful example of family reconstitution have been undertaken for Devon parishes by R.R. Sellman who has placed typescripts in WSL. The correct interpretation of the figures obtained is important. The researcher should be aware of the different types of averages: mean, median and mode, and the danger of generalising from small or unrepresentative samples. While pie charts and bar graphs can be attractive and have immediate impact, all too often the precise statistics on which they are based are not included and readers may require these for aggregative or comparative purposes. Care should be taken too in drawing the correct type of graph. Linear graphs are only appropriate where there is a true progression along the line. Thus if a series of settlements were ranked in population size a bar chart could be drawn to compare their populations; a line drawn through the population figures might create an aesthetic curve but would prove nothing.

### 5.4. COMPUTERS IN LOCAL HISTORY

The world of computers is a rapidly changing one but there are basically four ways in which the local historian may use computers:

Word processing of text.
This is essentially using the computer as a glorified typewriter with the ability to manipulate, move and edit blocks of text without retyping. Most standard word processing systems can accept text from other programs, either direct, or via an ASCII file which removes the special codes that individual programs use and so may lose special features such as tab columns or tables on transfer. Widely used programs include Word, Wordstar and AmiPro and some of these have special features to compile tables or indexes. Many word processing packages have the ability to incorporate scanned images and, together with the ability to use a variety of typefaces and page layouts, they are the equivalent of a desk-top publishing system.

Creation of databases.
This involves using the computer as a flexible filing system. Each entry (equivalent to a card record) is broken down into fields (equivalent to a line on an index card with a specific piece of information such a a per-

sonal name, occupation, or age). It is important to define the structure of each record so that information can later be searched for and sorted as required. Thus names should normally be inverted to bring the surname to the front and, if addresses are being stored in a series of fields, it is important that the town appears consistently in the same field in case sorting by town is required at a later date. There are two main types of fields, character and numeric. Numbers can be stored in character fields but it will not always be possible to perform calculations on them. Some database packages also have the ability to display scanned images, such as historic postcards, to which the database can then act as an index. Data can be moved from one database system to another, either directly or by converting the data into a special file where each field is delimited so that it can be recognised as a separate piece of data by the new program.

Development of spreadsheets.
This can be done where there is a considerable quantity of arithmetical data to be analysed. A change in any one box (cell) automatically updates the totals in specified columns without extensive recalculations by the researcher. Most spreadsheets are also linked to facilities for producing pie charts or bar charts.

Searching for information on networks.
With the development of the Internet much more information has become available, including a considerable amount of information of use to the local historian. Among such sites is the Genuki Project, based at Newcastle upon Tyne (http://www.cs.newcastle.ac.uk/genuki/DEV), which has included much information of genealogical and historical interest on all counties of the British Isles. Devon County Council has its own Internet pages (http://www.devon-cc.gov.uk), including information from the county local studies catalogue (http://www.devon-cc.gov.uk/library/locstudy). National providers of relevance to local historians include the Institute of Historical Research (http://www.ihr.sas.ac.uk) and the Royal Commision for Historical Manuscripts (http://www.hmc.gov.uk).

Further reading:
Bayley, N.J. *CAGe: computer aided genealogy* (1995)
Bradley, A. *Family history on your pc* (1996).
Edgington, S. *Micro-history: local history and computer projects* (1985).

# PART 6
# THE WORK OF LOCAL HISTORY SOCIETIES

### 6.1 Starting a Local History Society

If there is not already a local history society in your area you may wish to set one up. Broadly there are three ways in which a local history group gets started. The first is when a course of university extension lectures in a village or town has encouraged the formal setting up of a group to study in greater detail the history of a locality. The second, which may be a development of the first, is the desire to publish an account of the parish either in the form of a complete history or articles on various aspects of its past. Thirdly, and perhaps most frequently, there is an enthusiastic person, or persons, who encourage others to share their interest in what happened over the centuries in the area in which they live.

Assuming that the desire for a local history group exists, a first step must be to find out if there is any organisation doing similar work already. For example, is there a village or town 'civic society' which concerns itself with the past? Does the Parochial Church Council have any interest in or knowledge of the history of their church? Or the Parish Council? Is there a local Branch of the Devonshire Association or of the Devon Archaeological Society? Sometimes the Women's Institute preserves records donated by its members and so has information of value. If none of these bodies is doing the work of an LHS then the way is open to start a separate and special group but the co-operation of other groups is always worth having.

The aim of any LHS must be the study of its own and adjoining areas and the dissemination of the information that it accumulates. This should be stated clearly in its constitution or rules. But the aim does not impose limits on a group's activities since obviously your area will have been affected by what has happened elsewhere.

Any group tends to divide into those who want to be told the history of their village and those who wish to find it out for themselves. A division in fact between the supporters and the doers. To maintain a viable society it is essential to keep a balance between the two. The doers will probably have as their aim the publication of the results of their studies, while the more passive members will expect talks and outings, with no contribution expected from themselves. Experience has shown that a group of people brought together for the purpose, say, of writing a parish history tend to break up once the work is done. Equally a group dependent on a constant flow of speakers will find it increasingly difficult to maintain that flow. If the general aim of accumulating and disseminating knowledge of the history of a community is to be attained, there must be a compromise. The paragraphs that follow suggest some means to that end.

Whatever the reasons that lead to the decision to found an LHS, an early public meeting is essential. This meeting will establish likely membership, the inclinations of potential members, and possible income. It will also give some indication whether publication is a live issue. Supposing, then, that the launching ceremony is successful and that ad hoc officers and committee have been appointed, various issues will need to be agreed for presentation to the first annual general meeting for ratification. These are considered in the following paragraphs.

## 6.2. CONSTITUTION AND RULES

These should be as simple as possible but should include:
(a) Aims. Area to be studied and dissemination of information about it.
(b) Membership. Qualifications, types of membership, payment of subscriptions.
(c) AGM, quorum, election of officers and committee approval of subscription for following year and approval of accounts.
(d) Powers of officers and committee, co-option.
(e) Properties, funds, donations.
(f) Any special activities. Publications, lectures, resource collections
(g) Provisions for special meetings and winding up of the group.

The following rules are based, with permission, on those of the Uffculme Local History Group and provide an example for groups operating at a modest and not too complex level:

### Constitution

1. The objects of the Group shall be the promotion of and the study of the history of the parish of _____ and surrounding area and the dissemination of information on it through meetings, publications and other appropriate activities.

2. Membership shall be open to any interested person on payment of an annual subscription, the amount of which shall be determined at each Annual General Meeting.

3. An Annual General Meeting of the Group shall be held in _____ each year in the month of _____. A quorum shall be formed by ten or more members being present.

4. A Chairman, Secretary, Treasurer and three Committee members shall be elected at each Annual General Meeting to serve for one year. On the recommendation of the Committee, the Group may elect a President.

5. At each Annual General Meeting:

(i) The Secretary shall present minutes of the previous Annual General Meeting and a summary of the previous year's activities.

(ii) The Treasurer shall present, for formal adoption, a statement of the Group's membership and its financial position.

6. The Committee shall be responsible for day-to-day running of the Group and may take reasonable steps for the furtherance of its objects. They may co-opt up to three members to be responsible for particular projects or activities.

7. A Special Group Meeting may be called at any time at the request of two or more members of the Committee or ten or more members. The purpose of the Special Group Meeting shall be notified in writing by those requesting it. At least 14 days notice of any Special Group Meeting shall be given to members. A quorum shall be formed by ten or more members being present.

8. At all meetings of the Group, voting shall be by simple majority. In the event of a tied vote, the chairman of the meeting shall have an additional casting vote.

9. Any proposal for the winding-up of the Group and the disposal of its assets shall require the support of not fewer than 60% of members present at the Annual General Meeting or any Special Group Meeting at which the proposal is made. Any assets shall be distributed only to bodies with objects similar to those of the Group.

10. These rules may be amended only at an Annual General Meeting or Special group Meeting.

## 6.3 FINANCE

In setting up a group a certain amount of expenditure will be inevitable. Tactically it is better for the initiators to either give or advance the necessary cash than to approach, say, the Parish Council for help. Later you may need their aid for publication or for an exhibition. Councils and similar bodies are often reluctant to give twice!

In setting a subscription it is necessary to estimate probable expenditure. This is likely to fall under the following headings:
(a) Hire of meeting place.
(b) Secretarial and miscellaneous expenses.
(c) Advertising of meetings. This may include insertions in the Parish Magazine, for which some sort of financial contribution may be expected. Small posters on the parish and other notice boards are useful, and a printed version with a logo, if any, leaving blank space for particulars of meetings is worth considering.
(d) Speakers. Few groups are able to pay for professional speakers. While talks by people employed by local government are sometimes treated by them as duty visits, both they and private speakers should be offered travelling expenses which are normally 'petrol costs'. It is a welcome gesture if a light meal is offered to anyone coming from a distance.
(e) Publications. One essential publication is a card giving the year's programme of events and with names and addresses of officers and committee. The advantage of separating the costs of this and other publications from those of running the group is worth considering.
f) Exhibitions. This will vary considerably depending on whether the exhibition is a touring one for which the group will be responsible only for fixed charges such as insurance, or whether it is the group's own.
g) Outside visits. These can prove expensive, especially if transport is hired. It is prudent to make each visit self-supporting and, if a bus is booked, to get members' shares of the cost in advance!

## 6.4. ACTIVITIES

Sections 6.41 and 6.42 below are activities all groups will wish to be involved in. The other activities are special projects, many of which demand teamwork.

Further reading:
Rogers, A. (ed). *Group projects in local history.* (1977).

### 6.41. TALKS
In the early days of a group it is useful to have two kinds of talks: on general subjects and on the availability of sources. The first, for example, could cover the history of Devon agriculture, communications, landscape, industries etc. The second would describe published works and their availability and what is to be found in Record Offices and specialist libraries and how to use that material. You may be fortunate in having a member who has already done some work on the parish or there may be a neighbouring group, the history of whose parish is closely related to that of yours. But for the first couple of years or so there should be no lack of subjects to be handled by outside speakers.

### 6.42. VISITS
Apart from explanatory visits to Record Offices, museums etc, there is an advantage in seeing buildings and places with historical similarities to your own. Often there will be a LHG willing to help with the arrangements. If the group attracts a substantial membership, then distant visits become possibilities.

### 6.43 EXHIBITIONS
An exhibition on the general history of the village or a particular phase, if properly presented, is a useful advertisement for a Group. If it commemorates a particular event you may be able to secure the co-operation of the Parish and/or Parochial Church Councils. Much of the substance will generally be in the form of illustrations or diagrams. In the likely event of the Group not being able to afford modern presentation techniques, you will be dependent on the abilities of your members. If you have a register of material in private hands you may be able to persuade the owners to lend it but remember your liabilities to them. Insurance may be necessary, duty stewards while the exhibition is open will be essential. It should be noted too that the Record Office may be required by law to guard the exhibition so that records do not leave its custody.

Further reading:
Gray, V. and Liddell, B. *Running a local history fair.* (1989).

### 6.44. EDUCATIONAL AND OTHER COOPERATIVE LINKS

Schools may be less willing to help than in the past because of the demands of the national curriculum. Nevertheless schools normally have parish packs of historical information supplied by Devon Library Services and would probably welcome interested individuals who would be prepared to keep such packs in order and add to them. Indeed the school may be a useful base for the society, especially if members can be involved in giving talks to students. There are a wide range of other possibilities for co-operation, from joint meetings to the production of a historical map of the village.

### 6.45. ORAL HISTORY

This can be recorded by individual members or at a LHS meeting. If the latter, a topic should be chosen and a moderator appointed to guide the discussion. Arguably the collecting and preserving of local history is one of the most useful activities a group can perform.

Further reading:
Humphries, S. *The handbook of oral history: recording life stories.* (1984).
Marcombe, D. *Sounding boards: oral testimony and the local historian* (1996).
Thompson, P. *The voice of the past.* (1978).

### 6.46. RECORDING THE PRESENT

The reconstruction of the geography of the village at different periods is a fascinating if frustrating undertaking. The sources for such a study will have been described in the early talks and individuals can be encouraged to contribute the history of their own houses. Listed building should always be noted and an eye kept on structures which English Heritage might be asked to consider listing.

Further reading:
Brunskill, R.W. *Illustrated handbook of vernacular architecture.* (1971)
Norrington, V. *Recording the present* (1989).

### 6.47 INDEXING AND TRANSCRIBING

It is important that all members of teams that are involved in transcribing and indexing should be working to the same guidelines. There are various standards laid down but some conventions are generally accepted, for example the use of square brackets for supplying information which is not present in the original document, the use of dots, often in square brackets [...] to indicate material omitted in transcription. There are also various ways of expanding abbreviations. Examination of sample volumes of the new series of the Devon and Cornwall Record Society can show how these and other problems have been dealt with in a wide range of records.

Further reading:
Elliott, B.J. 'The problems of indexing a local newspaper.' *Local historian* 14:3 (1980) p.143-8.

### 6.48. LOCAL RESOURCE CENTRES

Inevitably the group will attract offers of objects of varying value and interest. Sometimes it will not be possible to refuse these without causing offence or without the item being destroyed. The storage of such things presents obvious problems and, unless a secure room or part of one can be found to store them, they will probably end up in some member's garage. A museum is not a practical proposition for an ordinary group but a secure storage place in which artefacts and records can be kept is always useful. Nevertheless the preservation of items which are a part of a village's past is important. One way of doing this is to establish a voluntary register and when an owner leaves the area to try to ascertain, as far as possible, what is going to happen to the items he or she is holding. By law some types of record, including parish records, have to be housed in a properly recognised record office and it is advisable for all original records to be transferred to safe custody. Arrangements can often be made for copies to be produced for local use.

### 6.49. PUBLISHING

This can make or break a group. Section 7 gives some indication of the range of possible publications and outlines some of the problems. The publication of a newsletter demands the services of an editor, access to a cheap source of duplication and a continuing supply of new material. The abilities of members in desk-top publishing or word processing can considerably reduce costs.

Further reading:
Banks, N. *Preservation of library materials.* (Newberry Library, 1978).
Moor, L.I. & A. *Conserving photographs.* (Bishopsgate press, 1978).

## 6.5. CONTINUITY

When a Local History Group is founded it should be the start of an association that will outlive its founders. To ensure this it should seek to establish itself as a normal part of village life, as usual as the football club or the Mothers' Union. This implies a broad-based membership, avoiding any implication that to belong any especial educational qualifications are required. The only qualification is an interest in the past. Given the current population trends in most Devon villages, many of the initial members will be incomers, most of them retired. While, inevitably, the latter will play a large part in organising the new society, it is vital that the 'old' villagers be involved in every stage of its development. It is on their knowledge that much of its work will be based. Remember that the LHG is not only recording the past for the present but is enabling the future to assess the present!

## 6.6 PUBLIC RELATIONS

Advertisement is important both to attract members and interest. Apart from obvious channels such as the parish magazine or local paper, if one exists, church fetes and similar events give opportunities for displays and the sale of publications, if available. It may be possible to raise cash as well as interest by medieval tombola or the like! The aim of publicity is two-fold: to add to your membership and to encourage fellow villagers to come to you with information of all kinds.

## 6.7 GENERAL

These notes are intended to be of help mainly to societies in small towns and villages. In most towns organisations already exist but that is no reason for not considering a new body for an individual parish, or to study a particular aspect of the town's history. Good luck - and don't forget to register your new society with The Devon History Society and with the County Local Studies Librarian.

Further reading:
Paget, M. *Running a local history society* (1988)

# PART 7
# WRITING LOCAL HISTORY

### 7.1. REFERENCES

Requirements for forms of reference vary but normally include the author, title, edition and date of publication for books, normally followed by the page reference in footnotes, and the author, title, periodical, issue, year and pages for periodical articles. The author's name is normally but not invariably inverted. Sometimes the place of publication and the publisher is also named and the imprint may be enclosed in parentheses. The publisher can normally give details of house style and there are manuals for editors. The result can have the following appearance:

Books:
Hoskins, W.G. *Local history in England.* 2nd ed. London: Longmans, 1972, pp. 174-176 or:
W.G. Hoskins, *Local history in England.* 2nd ed. (1972), 174-6.

Articles (the title of the article is in inverted commas, the title of the periodical or collection in italics:
W.J.Blake, 'Hooker's Synopsis Chorographical of Devonshire', *Trans. Dev. Assoc.,* 47 (1915), 334-68.
Joyce Youings, 'John Hooker and the Tudor bishops of Exeter', in M.Swanton (ed.) *Exeter Cathedral: a celebration* (1991), 202-7.

References can be grouped at the foot of each page, at the end of each chapter or at the end of the book. Avoid 'op. cit.' and 'ibid', prefer the author's name and date of publication as a brief means of reference to a separate bibliography or else refer back to earlier notes e.g. 'Hoskins (1972), 145.' or 'Evans (note 44), 134.'

An alternative form of reference, more normally used in scientific and archaeological publications is the Harvard system. Here the references are given in full in the body of the text thus: (Hoskins, 1972, 174-6) and the entries in the bibliography at the end of the work bring the date to the front in the form:

Hoskins, W.G. (1972) *Local history in England*, 2nd ed (London, Longman).

Further reading:
British Standard 1629: *Bibliographical references*
British Standard 5605: *Citing references*.

## 7.2. COPYRIGHT

It may be necessary to seek copyright clearance if substantial extracts of works are being quoted or recent illustrations are included in a publication. The whole question of copyright is very complex and there are a number of misunderstandings. For example a work does not have to be published to be in copyright and copyright is not dependent on the deposit of a copy in the British Library. The main copyright legislation is the Copyright Act 1988 but this has been amended by other legislation, notably by an EEC decree which extends the copyright term from fifty years to seventy years after the death of the author.

Further reading:
Wall, R.A. *Copyright made easier* (ASLIB, 1993).

## 7.3. PUBLICATION

There are many different forms of publication apart from books published by main-line publishers such as Phillimore or Devon Books. Publications can range from the single broadsheet through folded leaflets, and periodical articles to works in one or more volumes. There are also a variety of forms of publication and production methods available. Whatever the publication there are a number of factors that have to be considered:

Defining the scope of the publication. Will it cover the whole history of the parish or a particular period or topic? Will it be a reprint of an existing item, printed or manuscript, with or without a new introduction or commentary? A publication without a clearly defined scope tends to end up as a shapeless jumble of ill-digested snippets.

The end product envisaged. Is a published book intended or an article in a local or national periodical? Will it be part of a series? If so there may be existing guidelines on presentation to follow. Is an unpublished typescript the immediate intention? If so how many copies will be produced for the compilers, the village, libraries and museums? Will a master be held on computer. If so is it in a widely usable format (e.g. ASCII files)?

The organisation of the project. Will it be an individual or team task? If it is a team task specific duties have to be allocated to various team members (photography, interviewing, searching resources, indexing, keyboarding, editing etc).

Literature searching. It is vital not to duplicate research that has already been undertaken. Library catalogues, bibliographies and local collections of resources should be searched. An appeal through the parish magazine may unearth additional material. Any original archives discovered should be deposited in the Record Office.

Taking notes from sources. It is essential that full references are taken from each source consulted: author, title, publisher in the case of books or name of periodical in the case of periodical articles, date and page details. This information will be useful for the bibliography and references in the published volume. A note of the collection where the item was seen and the shelfmark will help if the item has to be consulted again.

Organising material. If the publication is a large one a filing system for the working papers is essential. The traditional card file is flexible and portable, A4 folders can house notes and photocopies and information can be put onto computer files (either word processed or as databases). Whatever method is used for storing information, adequate indexing is vital for retrieving it. Indexes by personal and place name, subject and sometimes date can all be useful.

Planning the finished work. As material is gathered, a list of sections or chapters will begin to emerge. These can be thematic or chronological in nature. An outline of the contents of each section can now be drawn up and keyboarding begun. Word processing or desk-top publishing can frequently cut typesetting costs by providing camera-ready copy and will also provide a tidy typescript from which a few copies can be run off, should publication prove to be impractical. When selecting material for the text it is important to avoid crowding the main text with too much detail. Some material, for example lists, can be relegated to appendices.

Further reading:
British Standard 5261: *Copy preparation and proof correction.*

Reference systems. These are essential for all but the most popular works. Footnotes can only be added at the final stage when the layout of individual pages is known. Endnotes, at the end of each chapter or of the book as a whole, can be added as work progresses but will frequently require renumbering. The Harvard system of referencing (the insertion of the author's surname, publication date and page in the text which refers to a bibliography at the end of the book) needs a minimum of updating but it is more obtrusive. See section 7.1 above.

Bibliography and indexes. The minimum reference for a bibliography is author, title, date for books, plus the title of the periodical, volume and page numbers for articles. See section 7.1 above. Indexes can greatly increase the reference value of a publication but is time-consuming and frequently has to be done in haste after the page proofs are available. It is important to decide what to index. As well as person and places, an index of subjects is useful. See section 5.2 above.

Further reading:
British Standard 3700 (ISO 999): *The preparation of indexes for books, periodicals and other publications.*

Levels of publication.
(a) FULL BOOK BY A COMMERCIAL PUBLISHER (e.g. Devon Books, Phillimore). Many publishers prefer to commission books, especially as part of a series. They may require reworking to fit in with their publication criteria. It is useful to contact publishers with a synopsis before writing; certainly look at other books by the publisher. Publishers will make strict judgments on commercial viability and you should expect some

delay in replies. The *Local History Magazine* book publishing service (01602-700369) is one means of publishing small local histories.

Devon Books, Official Publisher to Devon County Council, has embarked upon a series of local history publications, based on a standard format, in which they have worked closely with local history groups. The resultant books, concentrating largely on photographs collected from individuals within the community, contain captions and text written on themes such as social history, the church, transport, farming, etc. Works published to date include *Widecombe-in-the-Moor* (1996) and *The Cornwood Book* (1997). Devon Books liaises with the appropriate members of the community during the compilation of the work and oversees the design and production process. These works are published on subscription, with the publisher providing promotional flyers for circulation in order to secure pre-publication sales. Any group or individual wishing to discuss their intended publications in more detail can contact Devon Books for advice (01884 243242).

(b) VANITY PUBLISHING. This is to be avoided; it can be expensive but there are reputable publishers and printers who will handle material they consider good enough for publication. You pay the editorial and production costs and receive a finished product. Some publishers have facilities to publicise or assist in the distribution of such publications.

(c) SELF-PUBLISHED BOOK OR PAMPHLET. If you undertake publication yourself, a number of points have to be decided by you:

i. Format: what type size and page size will accommodate the information in a suitable number of pages? An estimate of the number of pages and details of illustrations is required before printers can provide costings.

ii. Binding style: stapled, spiral, comb, slide, perfect or sewn, paperback or hardback. Provision of an attractive cover can help sell a publication.

iii. Print-run: it is best to avoid being left with too many unsold copies. With laser printers and high-speed photocopiers, publication on demand is possible for specialist titles. Costs are considerably increased if the printer has to typeset from typescript and many printers will not even consider accepting manuscript. With publication on demand the author avoids committing too much money in advance, but the unit costs will be higher as the cost is the same for each copy produced and does not drop as when several hundred are run off a once.

iv. Costings: comparison can be obtained by approaching several local printers through the Yellow Pages. A very rough estimate of costs given by a local publisher in 1997 is that 1000 copies of a 100 page A5 format paperback book, with a single-colour cover, can cost £1500 although much will depend on the type of cover, the quality of paper and the use of colour illustrations. Lower print runs are possible but the 'run-on' costs are much lower than the 'set-up' costs. It should be recognised that smaller communities will only be able to support a relatively small print run.

v. Finance: this can be assisted by subscription publication (advertising for payment in advance, often at a reduced price) or by local sponsorship, either in the form of grants or loans.

vi. Copyright: this may need to be cleared on recent illustrations, maps or works from which extensive quotation is made, as well as unpublished archival material. On some non-copyright items obtained from collections reproduction fees may be charged.

ISBN (International Standard Book Number). This is used by booksellers and libraries for computerised ordering and cataloguing. It can help to circulate your publication more widely. The ISBN can be obtained free of charge from Whitaker, 12 Dyott Street, London WC1A 1DF. Ask for a publications notification form which will ensure that it is mentioned in the *Bookseller*, the national weekly trade periodical.

Legal deposit. One copy of each publication produced in the British Isles has to be forwarded to the Legal Deposit Office of the British Library, Boston Spa, Wetherby, West Yorkshire LS23 7BY. This will normally ensure its listing in the *British national bibliography*, which circulates internationally, but it may also result in a request for up to five more free copies from the agent for the other copyright libraries.

Setting a selling price. Take the unit print cost by dividing the total costs by the print run, remembering to make an allowance for six legal deposit copies, any complimentary or review copies, and a proportion of unsold copies. Also take into account inflation over two to three years, postage, bookseller's margin of at least 35 per cent and any profit (e.g. for the Church Restoration Fund, or the group's coffers). Set a price based on what is required to recover costs plus a reasonable profit. The print cost usually has to be at least doubled.

Publicity and distribution. Send copies to *Local Historian, Local History Magazine, Devon Historian* and other local or national periodicals for review, also to the County Local Studies Librarian who will include details in a fortnightly list of publications which is circulated to libraries throughout Devon for selection purposes. Details should have been circulated within the community and this is where the bulk of the sale would be expected. The local newspaper will often run a feature on the book, the author, or the society which may help sales, and the local radio may also be prepared to mention it, possibly interviewing the author. Make sure that the newspaper publishes sufficient details for readers to be able to obtain the item. Wider distribution is difficult and expensive. Booksellers in the larger towns may be persuaded to take a few copies but the majority of sales will often be through a direct approach to the author or a member of the group.

Shorter works (up to about 5000 words) may be more appropriate as a periodical article. For articles in periodicals you should attempt to see copies of the periodicals to ascertain the type of article they require and to read any advice for contributors which they may provide, especially regarding the length of contributions and their requirements for footnotes or references.

For unpublished typescripts at least two copies should be produced, one to be retained locally and the other to be placed in WSL.

A mixed form of publication is possible with the main text published as a booklet referring to the additional material which may be held as typescript notes, as microfiches inserted into the cover of the book, or made available as computer files on disk.

Further reading:
*Writers' and artists' yearbook* (annual)
Modern Humanities Research Association. *MHRA style book: notes for authors, editors and writers of dissertations*. 3rd ed. (1981).

Butcher, J. *Copy-editing: the Cambridge handbook for editors, authors and publishers* (3rd ed, 1992)

Dymond, D. *Writing local history: a practical guide* (1988)

Hart, H. *Hart's rules for compositors and readers at the University Press, Oxford* (39th ed, 1983)

Marius, R. *A short guide to writing about history* (2nd ed, 1995)

Hampshire County Library. *Publishing for local history: guidance for the budding author* (1995).

# INDEX

references refer to the section numbers

# NOTES